ATLAS

OF

extreme weather

LORENZO PINI

JONGLEZ PUBLISHING

Contents

Beaufort
Sea

Arctic Circle

Alaska
(USA)
Fairbanks

Anchorage

Hudson
Bay

Churchill

CANADA

Ontario

Calgary

Winnipeg

Rainy
River

Vancouver

Seattle

Minnesota

Montréal

Toronto

Chicago

New

UNITED STATES OF AMERICA

Pacific
Ocean

Atl
Oc

MEXICO

N

Hailstorm Alley · Alberta, Canada

Hailstorms are so frequent that a specialised company resorts to 'cloud seeding' to reduce their impact

On 13 June 2020, a devastating storm of hailstones the size of golf balls and 100 km/h winds hit the city of Calgary in the province of Alberta, Western Canada. The damage was devastating: more than 70,000 homes and vehicles, along with entire crops, were destroyed. Damage amounted to an estimated $1.2 billion, making it the fourth costliest natural disaster in Canadian history.

Hailstorms of this magnitude have affected many places on the planet throughout history, but the geographical area around Calgary has an unenviable record for the frequency of the phenomenon. In fact, the area is known as 'Hailstorm Alley'.

Every summer, from the end of May to mid-September, this area of Alberta, east of the Canadian Rockies, between High River (65 km south of Calgary) and Lacombe (175 km north of Calgary), averages more than 20 hailstorms, half of which are medium to severe.

To name just a few examples, Calgary was also hit by heavy hail in September 1991 and July 2010, Airdrie, Red Deer and Rocky Mountain House in August 2014, Ponoka in June 2016, Lacombe in May 2017 and much of central Alberta in July 2018.

What causes such adverse weather? As usual, it is necessary to start with the geographical characteristics of the area. Hailstorm Alley is located on a bare plateau at about 1,000 metres above sea level. It is very cold in winter, but temperatures can warm up very quickly in summer (Calgary's heat record, set in August 2018, was 36.5°C). In the middle hours of summer days, under the sun, a heat bubble expands on the plateau, and toward the west, colliding with the slopes of the Canadian Rockies. Warm air is suddenly forced up (the mountain range is more than 3,000 metres), cooling and condensing to form massive cumulonimbus clouds. Once they have reached higher altitudes, the convective clouds are pushed east again by the winds at altitude and return toward Hailstorm Alley charged with energy.

Under normal conditions, thunderstorms develop without hail, but when arctic air at altitude infiltrates this orographic dynamic (which is very frequent, given Alberta's exposure to northern winds), thermal contrasts become even more pronounced and menacing cumulonimbus clouds form of more than 10 km high. Updrafts in these kinds of clouds are very strong. Instead of falling as rain, the water droplets at the base of the cloud are sent at great speed toward the upper levels of the cloud, where they freeze, turn into spheres of ice and, because of their weight, fall to the ground through the force of gravity. This is how hail forms.

When the energy at play is extreme, as is the case in the meteorological–geographical context of central Alberta, ice balls can make several journeys within the cloud, clumping together and forming larger and larger spheres, reaching diameters of more than 5 cm, and even 10 cm.

Canadian insurance companies were faced with continuous hail damage claims and in 1996, determined to find a solution, they founded the Alberta Severe Weather Management Society (ASWMS) and financed the Alberta Hail Suppression Project (AHSP). That was the start of the cloud seeding that operates 24/7 from 1 June to 15 September. When weather radars intercept potential hail clouds, aircraft based in Calgary and Red Deer fly around the cumulonimbus releasing silver iodide and dry ice (solid-state CO_2) into it. This chemical composition promotes the formation of condensation nuclei and accelerates the creation of ice crystals, interrupting the cycle which produces large hail.

Cloud seeding does not work every time, though. Wind can render the process useless. But, even when partially effective, it can at least limit the size of the hailstones and render them almost harmless.

Cloud seeding prompts much discussion and criticism. It has been adopted in various countries, including to cause rain or snow. According to the American Chemical Society, cloud seeding in Alberta was able to reduce hailstorm damage by 27 per cent, but some studies point out that the use of silver iodide must be measured to ensure it does not become toxic.

The worst freezing rain in recent history · Quebec

In January 1998, the area between the USA and Canada was hit by a 'perfect' ice storm that transformed everything into a surreal, glass-like landscape

Of all ice-related atmospheric phenomena, freezing rain is among the most feared due to its ability to bring down trees and electrical infrastructure, tear down roofs, and render roads impassable.

It can occur in winter in continental areas along the temperate and sub-polar belts, especially in the Great Plains of the USA, Canada, central Europe, and Russia.

Freezing rain forms when particularly moist and warm air flows over a layer of frozen air. The heavier frozen air remains 'stuck' to the ground. This creates a thermal inversion condition: at high altitude, temperatures are positive, and it rains, while temperatures at ground level remain at or below zero degrees. The instant the raindrops hit the ground they freeze and form a layer of ice, similar to a glass film, that covers every surface.

If the rain is persistent (for hours or even days), the consequences can be devastating. This was the case during the most extreme freezing rain event in recent history, in January 1998 in an area between the American Great Lakes and the St Lawrence River valley in Quebec, Canada.

What became known as 'the great ice storm of 1998' began on 4 January, when deep, low pressure originated south of the American Great Lakes, drawing warm, moist air from the Gulf of Mexico. At the same time, high pressure over Labrador maintained a flow of icy eastern air in the lower layers. The collision of conflicting air masses produced a widespread disturbance which could not progress east due to high pressure in the Atlantic Ocean blocking its path. Unfortunately, this provided all the elements for the 'perfect' ice storm.

The worst affected area was the province of Montérégie in Quebec, south-east of Montreal. More than 100 mm of freezing rain fell in the triangle between Saint-Hyacinthe, Saint-Jean-sur-Richelieu and Granby, turning everything into a surreal, glass-like landscape.

The accumulation of ice caused 76 high-voltage pylons and thousands of wooden power line poles to collapse, and hundreds of transformers to explode. Despite several breaks, the rain persisted until 9 January. By then, 300,000 residents of the area were left without electricity, being plunged into the dark with no heating. The media coined the term 'Black Triangle'.

Thousands of tree branches littered the ground, and no one could drive in the streets or walk on the pavements. People found shelter in facilities equipped with electric generators, like schools or gyms, in the hope electricity would be restored soon, but it took almost a month.

In the meantime, administrations within the 'Black Triangle' provided firewood, and the supply of small domestic gas generators was encouraged. The army intervened to clean up the streets and distribute supplies.

Along with the Montérégie region, the great ice storm of 1998 also severely affected the large cities of Ottawa and Montreal and the US states of New York, Vermont, New Hampshire and Maine. There were 46 deaths and damage totalled $6 billion.

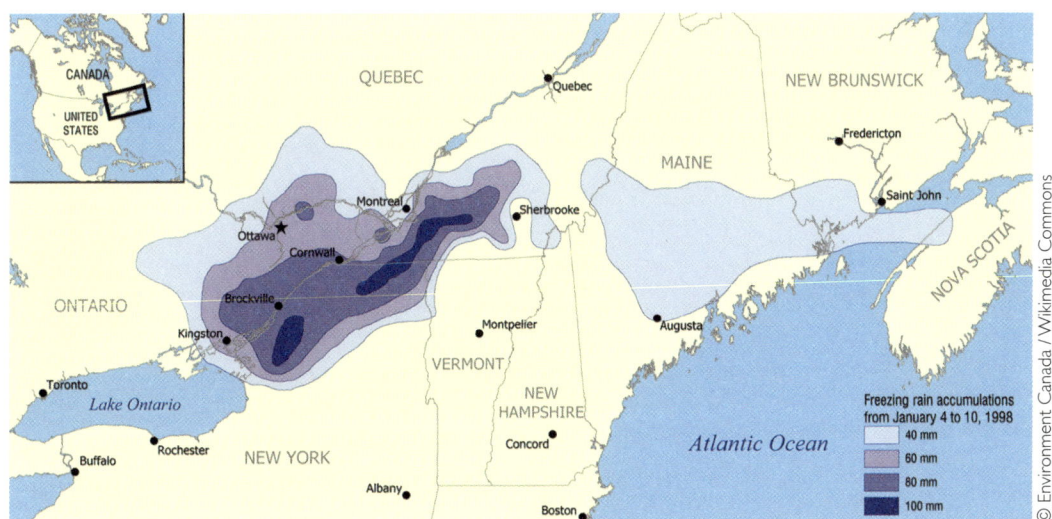

Greenland
(DENMARK)

*Baffin
Bay*

*Beaufort
Sea*

*Labrador
Sea*

Arctic Circle

Fairbanks
○

100°

*Hudson
Bay*

Churchill
○

CANADA

Calgary
○

Winnipeg
○

Vancouver
○

Seattle
○

Montréal
○

Toronto
○

*Avalon
Peninsula*

Chicago
○

New York
○

**UNITED STATES
OF AMERICA**

*Pacific
Ocean*

*Atlantic
Ocean*

MEXICO

CUBA

N

VENEZUELA

COLOMBIA

1 000 km

Avalon Peninsula · Newfoundland, Canada

The fog factory: 206 days of fog a year

The shape of Avalon Peninsula resembles a five-pointed star thrown out into the Atlantic. It loosely hangs from Newfoundland Island by an isthmus barely 5 km wide. It gives the impression of always being on the verge of setting off into the ocean. Perhaps it is trying to escape the extreme weather in this corner of Canada. Despite being on the same latitude as Paris, the peninsula's climate is much more hostile.

The wind on the island of Newfoundland is relentless, the sky is overcast four days out of five, snow and rain are abundant, and tropical storms and hurricanes pass through. In fact, cyclones from the tropical belt of the Atlantic are often sucked in by the Gulf Stream and flow close to the eastern coasts of the US, lapping them from south to north until they reach Newfoundland, especially its eastern part.

The most extreme weather phenomenon, however, is fog. In fact, the Avalon area, and in particular the village of Argentia, holds the world's highest average number of foggy days per year, with an impressive 206.

Just off the coast of Newfoundland, two ocean currents with opposite characteristics meet: the cold Labrador current and the warm Gulf Stream current. The closest point of contact with the mainland occurs just off the Avalon Peninsula. The opposite thermal characteristics of the waters interact with the layers of air above. The milder, wetter air that accompanies the Gulf Stream flows over the colder layer generated by the Labrador flow and, like a mirror when taking a shower, thick condensation forms. Extensive blankets of fog initially form over the Grand Banks of Newfoundland – a shallow-water system known for its exceptional abundance of fish east of the island. Local winds and the orography determine how the fog drifts and how persistent it is. The fog is more pronounced near the coast around Argentia (in contrast, inland areas of Newfoundland are usually sunnier).

The complex interactions between ocean currents and atmospheric turbulence, as well as physical and thermodynamic processes ranging from vapour saturation to radiation, make fog forecasts extremely complex and unreliable. This is why, in 2018, the US and Canadian governments funded the C-FOG (coastal fog) project in Newfoundland. The aim of the field research, coordinated by engineer Joseph Fernando, was to dispel the mysteries of fog and limit its impact on air and ship traffic.

Baffin
Bay

Beaufort
Sea

**Alaska
(USA)**   Fairbanks ○   Arctic Circle

Anchorage ○   Hudson
                                                      Bay

                                      Churchill ○

                                  CANADA

                  Calgary ○   *Snowbelts*

Vancouver ○   Winnipeg ○   Montréal ○
       ○ Seattle   Toronto ○
                                      Chicago ○
                                                         ○ New York

Pacific
Ocean   **UNITED STATES
                                    OF AMERICA**

                                                              Atlantic
                                                              Ocean

**Hawaii
(USA)**

                        MEXICO   CUBA

N

                                                              VENEZU

                                                              COLOMBIA

1 000 km

The 'snowbelts' of the American Great Lakes · US

Impressive snowstorms generated by the so-called 'lake effect'

Among the countless snowfalls on Earth, those around the American Great Lakes deserve a special mention due to their magnitude and dynamics.

Meteorologists have coined the term 'snowbelts' to identify seven areas distributed along the southern and western shores of the five lakes (Superior, Michigan, Huron, Erie, Ontario) between Canada and the US. These areas are exposed to very substantial snowstorms caused by the so-called 'lake effect'.

From November, icy currents move south from the Canadian Arctic, reaching the Great Lakes unhindered. The cold north-westerly winds blow over the lake surfaces and, at that time of year, the lakes are not yet frozen, providing moisture and warmth. The colder, heavier air literally undermines the warmer air on the lakes, forcing it to rise abruptly and triggering the development of convective clouds.

The clouds are carried by the wind toward the opposite shores, to the southern and western sectors, where they thicken as they come up against the first hills. This creates real cloud bands, similar to long ribbons, filled with precipitation, ready to pour ashore in the form of sudden snowstorms. These snowstorms can lead to 'whiteout' conditions that create a total lack of visibility due to the combination of snow lifted by the wind and snow from the sky.

Lake-effect snowfalls can be as intense as they are localised: very often, within a few hundred metres, you can go from a blizzard to sunshine and back. This causes great inconvenience to motorists.

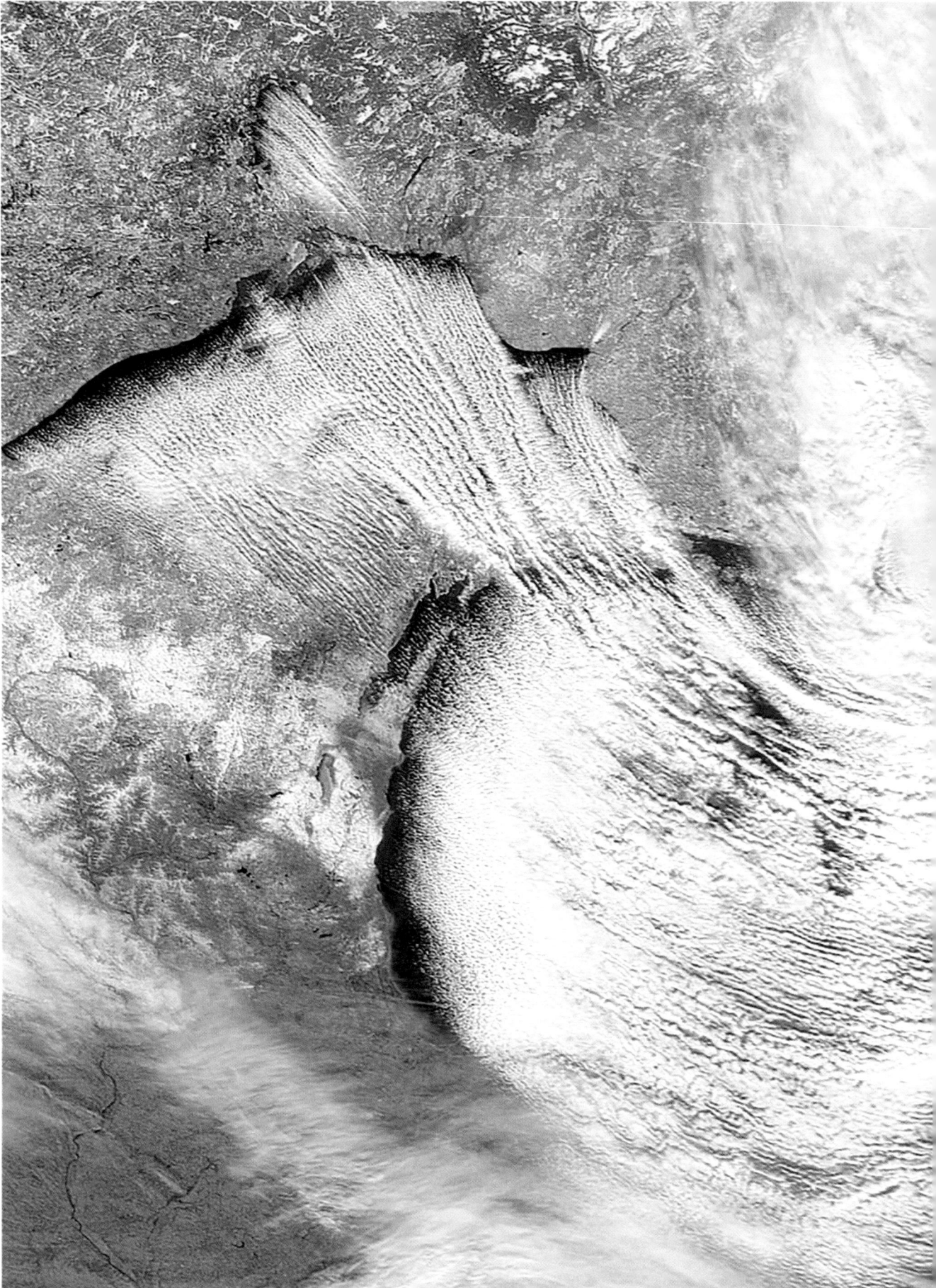

Among the seven snowbelts, the one with the highest average annual snowfall accumulation is located between Lakes Erie and Ontario, along a line connecting the cities of Buffalo, Rochester and Syracuse. As much as 75 cm of snow can fall in 24 hours in these locations, and hourly highs of 28 cm have been recorded.

A few recent episodes show the magnitude of this weather pattern. Between 29 November and 2 December 1976, more than 100 cm of snow paralysed Buffalo, and during that winter the city set its own seasonal record with 507 cm of snowfall. On 13 March 1993, the historic 'Superstorm' poured 110 cm of snow on Syracuse in two days, while in November 2022 more than 2 metres of snow fell in three days in the town of Hamburg, just south of Buffalo.

In this densely populated area – with more than half a million inhabitants – weather forecasts become crucial to prevent danger. Advanced weather radars make it possible to monitor the formation of cloud bands over the lakes, so timely warnings can be issued. Also, it is well known that the maximum intensity of snowstorms occurs between late autumn and early winter, when the lake waters are still at a high temperature and contribute more to the instability of incoming cold air masses.

In this sense, global warming contributes to even more extreme phenomena. Longer summers raise the waters of the Great Lakes to 1–2 °C above average. This means the thermal contrast in the autumn is more pronounced and increases clouds and precipitation. In the heart of winter, when the surface of the lakes tends to freeze over, snow continues to fall but is less abundant since there is no more evaporation on the lake surface.

The inhabitants are familiar with this extreme climate and know that, in certain conditions, there is nothing to do but wait for the bad weather to pass. In the Great Lakes snowbelts, news of snowfalls capable of paralysing cities for a whole week anywhere else on the planet are met with a shrug and a certain sense of pride.

The Golden Snowball Award

The Golden Snowball Award, a competition held annually between the cities of Buffalo, Syracuse, Rochester, Binghamton and Albany, celebrates the amount of snow accumulated in winter. At the end of spring, great festivities are held and the snowiest location is voted the winner. In the 1980s, at the height of the event, thousands of spectators flocked to witness the awards, bands performed and representatives from places around the world famous for snowfall were invited. In 2022–23, the award was presented to Buffalo, with its 334 cm of snow accumulation. But the real rivalry between the cities is not so much snow accumulation as the ability to clean up the streets and resume normal life after a storm as quickly as possible.

Paradise Inn · US

Holder of the world record for snow accumulation in a single year:
31 metres in 1971–72

The human-inhabited place on Earth with the largest snowfall is probably not where you think. While you may naturally look to the poles and Arctic (or Antarctic), this is the first mistake to avoid; the coldest parts of the world lack the moisture needed for intense precipitation.

It is also reasonable to think that record-breaking snowfalls occur in villages in the world's highest mountains, such as the Himalayas or the Andes. This too would be wrong. While it is true that above 4–5,000 metres every mountain range receives several metres of snow each winter, it is equally true that altitude is not enough to provide an exact answer.

The geographical characteristics necessary for heavy and regular snowfall require high humidity, intense jet streams, and a particular way of cooling the air. All of these criteria are found in the coastal mountain ranges in the temperate belts of the northern hemisphere and exposed to the western ocean currents. To pinpoint the answer, the perfect mountains for record-breaking snowfall are in the western US, between British Columbia, Oregon, Washington State and Northern California.

The relentless, humid currents from the Pacific, real 'trains' of water vapour, brush up against the slopes of these mountain ranges. They bar the way forward, and the humid currents have no choice but to shed their rainy and snowy contents.

One of the areas most exposed to this configuration is the Cascade Range, which reaches its highest elevation point at Mount Rainier (4,394 metres). Within the national park of the same name, on the southern slope of the mountain at an altitude of 1,600 metres, is the Paradise Inn lodge. This iconic wood and stone hotel, built in the Alpine style in 1916, was declared a national monument and is still a reference point for skiers and hikers. Beyond its vintage charm, the Paradise Inn is famous for holding the world record for snow accumulation in a single year. Between 19 February 1971 and the same day in 1972, Paradise's meteorological station recorded a whopping 31.5 metres of snow.

The hotel is only open from May to September, but during the winter months it is maintained by a tunnel connected to the front door. If the weather permits, it is possible to walk along the road that leads there even during the cold season, between walls of snow as high as buildings, until you reach the hotel's car park, whose second-floor windows emerge from the surrounding 'white ocean' that covers everything. The average annual snowfall in the Paradise Inn area is around 15 metres, with total accumulations on the ground of up to 9 metres at the end of the season (the fallen snow compacts, melts or evaporates, so the centimetres fallen never match the ground accumulation).

The secret of such heavy snowfall lies in the combination of several factors: the powerful, relentless westerly currents from the Pacific reaching the Cascade Range filled with moisture along with the mountains, which are high enough to act as a barrage, push the air up, cooling it and forcing steam particles to condense into clouds loaded with snow crystals. An additional factor is the location of the Paradise Inn, which stands right in front of the mass of Mount Rainier. The 4,400-metre mountain further slows the eastward progression of the weather fronts. As a result, they can persist for several days over the same area and produce extraordinary amounts of snow.

The Pineapple Express

The coastal areas of the western US are exposed to very rich flows of water vapour, known as 'atmospheric rivers'. One of the most famous is the 'Pineapple Express', a very long corridor of slow-moving currents from west to east, capable of transporting large amounts of moisture from Hawaii to the North American coast. These currents sometimes cause flooding rains and very heavy snowfall on the exposed slopes of the Rocky Mountains.

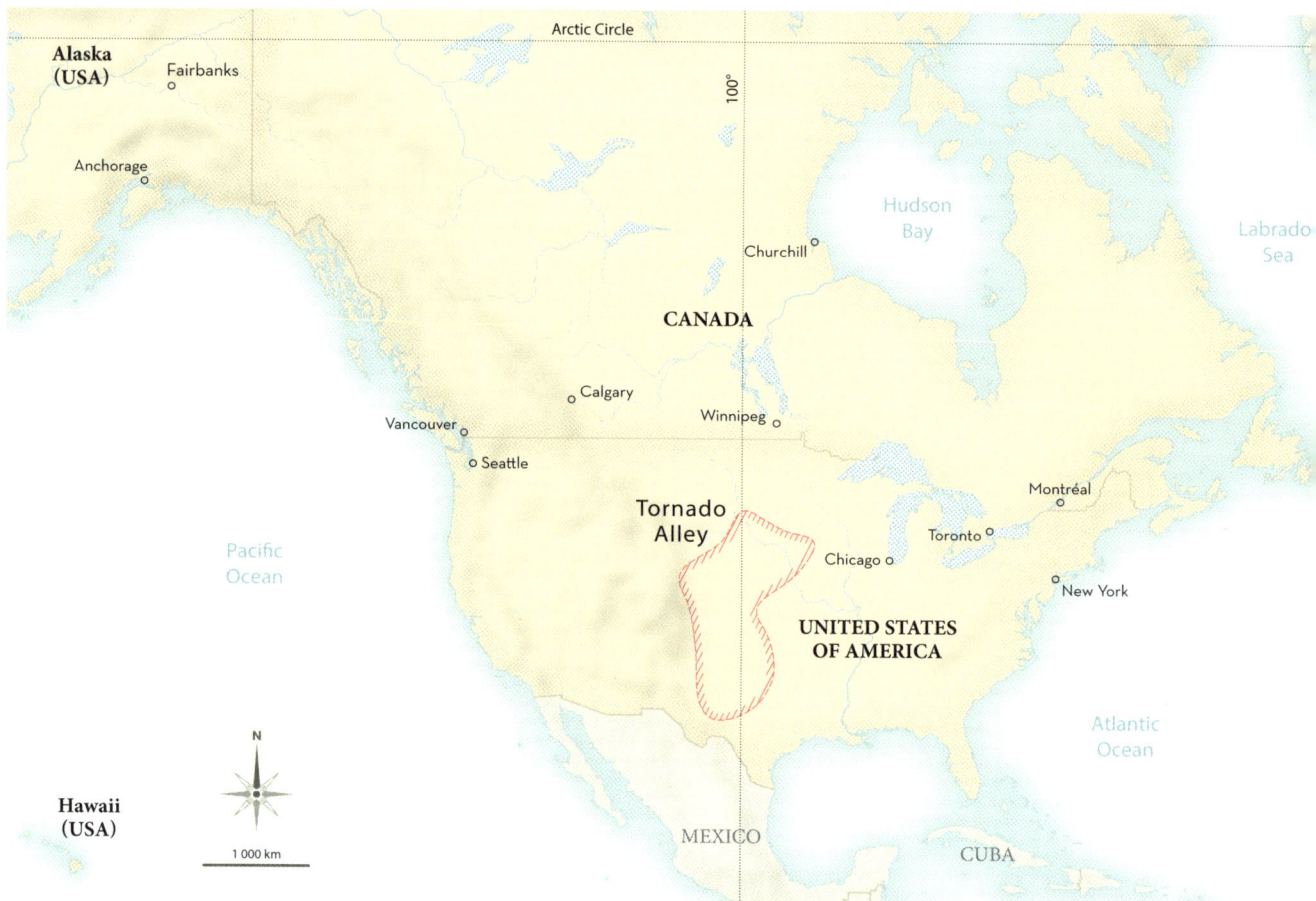

Arctic Circle

Alaska
(USA)

Fairbanks

Anchorage

CANADA

Churchill

Hudson
Bay

Labrador
Sea

Calgary

Winnipeg

Vancouver

Seattle

Montréal

Toronto

Tornado
Alley

Chicago

New York

Pacific
Ocean

UNITED STATES
OF AMERICA

Atlantic
Ocean

N

Hawaii
(USA)

1 000 km

MEXICO

CUBA

100°

Tornado Alley · US

Hundreds of tornadoes every spring

The term 'Tornado Alley' comes from the Spanish verbs 'tornar' (to turn) and 'tronar' (to thunder), which is exactly what happens when a column of air is created between the heart of a thundercloud and the ground as it rotates violently, razing to the ground everything in its path.

Tornadoes can form in many parts of the planet, but it is in the central belt of the US, aptly named Tornado Alley, that they occur most frequently, with around a thousand per season.

The reason for this lies in the geographical configuration and the size of the US, especially the Great Plains of the Midwest and the South. They are not sheltered by mountain ranges and form the meeting point between Arctic currents, winds from the Pacific and warm, humid air rising from the Gulf of Mexico.

The combination of these different air masses can generate, between spring and early summer, intense thunderstorm activity, an essential trigger for the dreaded tornadoes.

Tornado Alley is a vast area from South Dakota to Texas along the 100th meridian line, which marks a clear divide in the US climate. Between April and May (but sometimes also in March and June), when cooler, drier air descending from the north-west collides with warm, moist air over the Great Plains, particularly violent thunderstorm systems called 'supercells' can develop.

Within a supercell, the warm currents rising from the ground toward the heart of the cloud (known as 'updrafts') can take on a rotating component and become vortexed. This is due to the nature of the winds – which are opposite in terms of direction and speed – blowing between the base and the top of the cloud. The rotational motion created within the supercell is called a 'mesocyclone', a spiral where the pressure drops abruptly, capable of feeding itself by sucking in colder air from the advanced part of the thunderstorm. As the colder air condenses below the base of the cumulonimbus, the vortex 'escapes' from the heart of the cloud, and a kind of funnel builds toward the ground. If the vortex is structured well enough to reach the ground, it becomes a tornado.

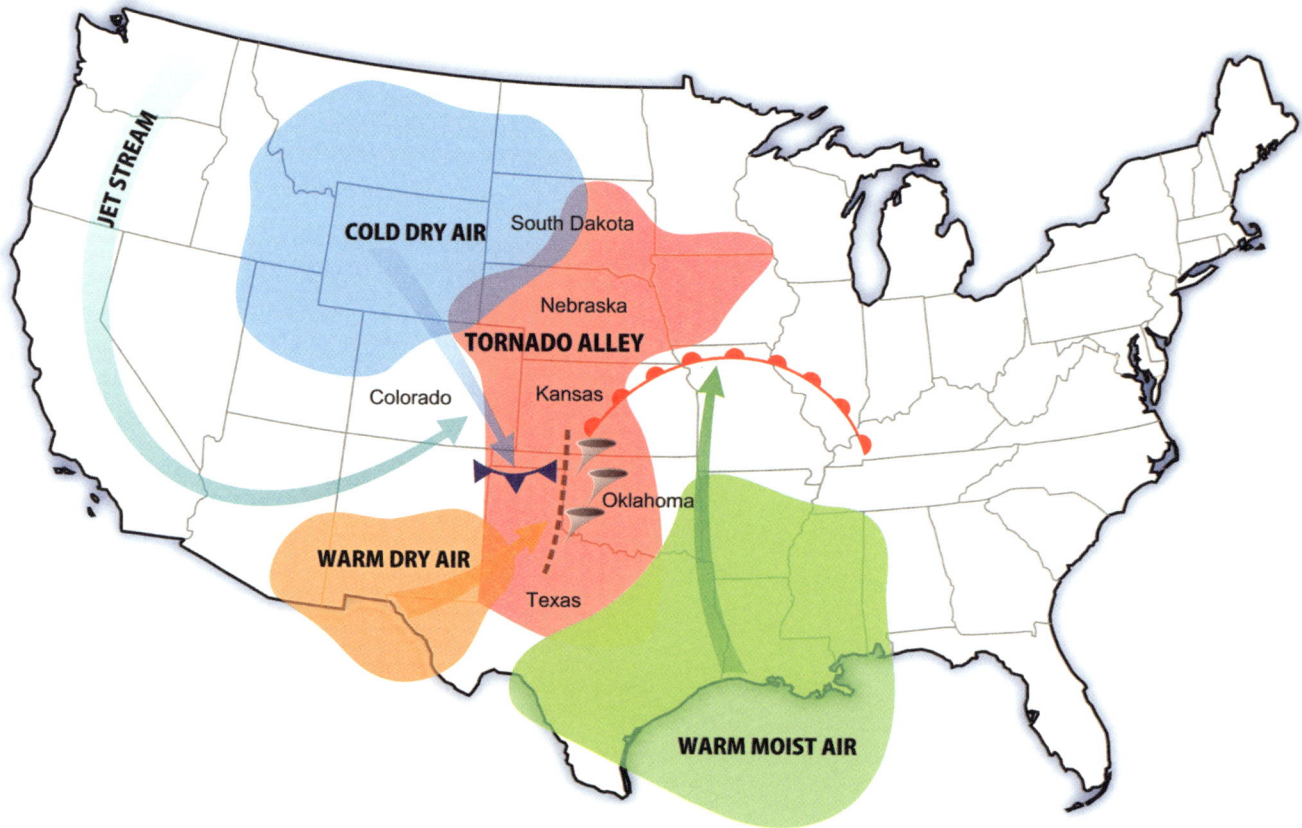

COLD DRY AIR

South Dakota

JET STREAM

Nebraska

TORNADO ALLEY

Colorado

Kansas

Oklahoma

WARM DRY AIR

Texas

WARM MOIST AIR

The most catastrophic tornado of all time

Tornadoes are classified by the Fujita scale into five categories (F0 to F5) based
on the damage they cause. The most devastating ones have winds of up to 500 km/h
at their epicentre, a diameter of up to 300 metres, and cover distances of tens of kilometres.
The most catastrophic tornado of all time occurred on 18 March 1925 between Missouri,
Illinois and Indiana. The so-called 'Great Tri-State Tornado' formed at 1 p.m. near Ellington,
Missouri, and moved north-east at a speed of about 110 km/h. At the Illinois border it gained
even more power, reaching an estimated 482 km/h. Because it moved so quickly,
eyewitnesses said they were not able to distinguish the vortex, but instead saw a cloud that
came down and devoured their homes. Whatever lay in the path of the tornado was
completely destroyed. After devastating Missouri, it killed almost 550 people in just 40 minutes
in Illinois, 234 of them in the town of Murphysboro, which to this day remains the place in the
US with the most deaths from a single tornado. But the tornado was not over: the Tri-State
Tornado reached as far as Indiana, razing the town of Princeton to the ground, before dissipa-
ting at about 4.30 p.m. In three and a half hours it had covered 352 km and claimed 695 lives.
Over the last two decades, global warming has not only increased the number and frequency
of tornadoes, but also changed, to some extent, their main route. The boundary between the
arid and green belts represented by the 100th meridian is shifting about 200 km to the east.
Along with Tornado Alley, the Dixie Alley between Mississippi, Arkansas, Alabama, Tennessee
and Florida is another vast area where this extreme weather event now occurs frequently.

The 100th meridian

If we look at a map of North America, west of the 100th meridian the ground is brown,
symbolising arid steppes, while the east is dominated by the green of the prairies and corn
crops. In fact, the arid western belt suffers from the rainfall shadow cast by the
Rocky Mountains, which blocks Pacific disturbances, while states to the east benefit
from the moist currents from the south (Gulf of Mexico) and west (Atlantic Ocean).
As a result, the states of Oklahoma and Texas, straddling the 100th meridian where the
two different climatic zones meet, are often victims of the violent exchanges of energy.

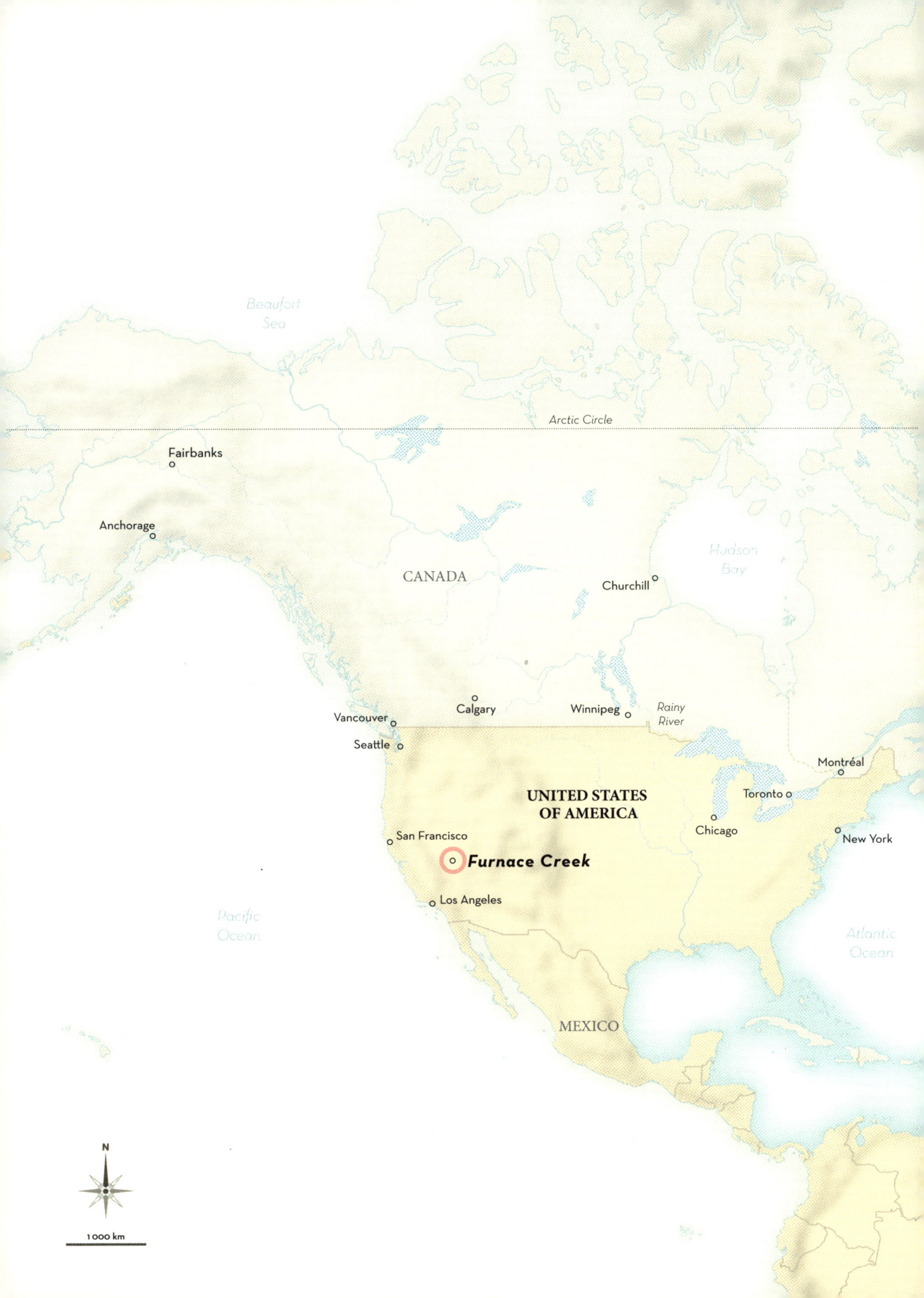

Beaufort
Sea

Arctic Circle

Fairbanks

Anchorage

CANADA

Churchill

Hudson
Bay

Vancouver

Calgary

Winnipeg

Rainy
River

Seattle

UNITED STATES
OF AMERICA

Montréal

Toronto

San Francisco

Chicago

New York

Furnace Creek

Los Angeles

Pacific
Ocean

Atlantic
Ocean

MEXICO

N

1 000 km

Furnace Creek · Death Valley, US

The highest temperature ever recorded: 56.7°C

Parts of North Africa, the Arabian Peninsula, Iran, Pakistan and Australia can exceed the 50°C threshold. But it is in the US, and in particular in Death Valley, that this extreme temperature is markedly exceeded every summer. Furnace Creek, the gateway to Death Valley Natural Park, holds the record for the highest temperature ever recorded.

In this Californian location, which is now the site of a visitor centre for tourists, the weather station recorded an astonishing 56.7 °C on 10 July 1913.

Death Valley is a desert area below sea level. It is a brackish basin that originated from the drying up of a sea that existed in the Palaeozoic Era. Badwater Basin, the lowest point in the park, is at minus 86 metres, while Furnace Creek is at minus 58 metres. About two hours' drive west of Las Vegas, Death Valley lies at the same latitude (36°N) as Gibraltar and Tokyo but experiences only 50 mm of average annual rainfall, less than the driest areas of the Sahara.

What has the greatest influence on summer temperatures is the morphology of the valley. It is a long and narrow basin surrounded by steep mountain ranges that on the western side exceed 3,000 metres, blocking the way for humid Pacific currents. The clear, dry air and sparse vegetation cover allow sunlight to warm the desert surface. The heat radiated by the rocks and the scorching ground is unable to dissipate, trapped deep in the valley (at Zabriskie Point, 300 metres higher than Furnace Creek, the highs stop at 42–45 °C, which is extreme but not record-breaking).

When night falls and the sunshine begins to disappear, the air in contact with the mountain slopes cools rapidly and, having become heavier, it tends to drift down from the ridges toward the basin below. The mountain breezes then set in, which slightly dampen the heat bubble above Furnace Creek. Even so, the lows in July and August struggle to fall below 30°C.

For those who like numbers, here are a few figures that give an idea of the hellish climate in Furnace Creek. Since the Furnace Creek weather station has been recording data, the 130°F (54.5°C) threshold has only been reached, apart from the record-breaking day of 1913, in 2020 and 2021 (usually the peaks are between 48°C and 52°C). The highest number of consecutive days with a maximum temperature of 38°C or above was 154 in the summer of 2001, while the summer of 1996 had 40 days above 48°C and 105 days above 43°C. The summer of 1917 had 43 consecutive days with a temperature of 48°C or higher.

And the rest of the year? Outside the May to September period, Death Valley is a pleasant place to visit. In winter and spring, daytime temperatures stay between 15°C and 22°C, and at night it rarely gets close to zero (the record low was -10°C, again in 1913). Although there is very little rain, there may be a few brief showers during the cooler months. They are followed by the blooming of the desert.

In 2005, an exceptional flood occurred in Death Valley, causing the reappearance of what used to be Lake Manly some 20,000 years ago. On that occasion, some park rangers set a new record: crossing the desert in a canoe. In the following days, the lake evaporated rapidly, leaving behind a mixture of mud and salt.

© Forestangels / Pixabay

HONDURAS

Caribbean Sea

NICARAGUA

COSTA
RICA   PANAMA

Catatumbo

VENEZUELA

GUYANA   FRENCH
                GUIANA

COLOMBIA   SURINAME

Galapagos
(ECUADOR)   ECUADOR

PERU   BRAZIL

*Pacific
Ocean*   BOLIVIA

                    PARAGUAY

                                        *Atlantic
                                        Ocean*

CHILE   URUGUAY

        ARGENTINA

                    Falkland Islands
                    (Islas Malvinas)
                    (U.K.)

                                        South Georgia
                                        (U.K.)

N

1 000 km

Catatumbo · Venezuela

The most electric place on the planet,
with thousands of lightning strikes for at least 250 nights a year

One of the greatest weather phenomena on the planet takes place where Lake Maracaibo meets the Catatumbo river. Two out of three nights the sky above the lake is torn apart by an average of 280 lightning bolts per hour. Most of the thunderbolts are cloud-to-cloud types and visible up to 300 km away.

The intensity and frequency of these electrical storms can be attributed to two factors. The first is the geography of the place. Lake Maracaibo is located in the tropical belt close to the Caribbean Sea and is surrounded to the west by the Sierra de Perijá and to the east by the Andes. The geography acts as a funnel that channels the hot, humid winds from the sea. When the warm air meets the slopes of the mountains surrounding the lake, it is forced to rise abruptly, cooling as it gains altitude to the point of condensation. This triggers the classic mechanism that leads to the formation of convective clouds and then thunderstorms, a pattern that is practically uninterrupted here. The second factor acts as an amplifier: methane rising from the decomposing organic material in the Catatumbo delta fuels the mechanism that activates electrical discharges in the clouds and boosts the long sequence of lightning strikes.

© Cesar sanchez007 / Wikimedia Commons

The 'Catatumbo lightning', as the atmospheric phenomenon is called, has been documented since the late 16th century.

In his epic poem *La Dragontea* (1598), Spanish playwright and novelist Lope de Vega discussed the decisive role lightning played in the story of Sir Francis Drake. The English privateer wanted to conquer Maracaibo, but lightning illuminated the night and revealed his intentions, sending them up in smoke. Throughout history, the constant recurrence of the flashing thunderstorm was a point of reference for sailors, like a beacon from hundreds of kilometres away.

Lightning on Lake Maracaibo has always attracted tourists from all over the world. Until the 2000s, the best place to observe the phenomenon was Congo Mirador, a small island which is home to a few fishermen's stilt houses in the south-west corner of the lake. After the opening of a new canal, however, the village was silted up and abandoned. From Congo Mirador, many moved to nearby Ologá, which is now the best location for 'lightning hunters'. This is also a small fishing village with 46 stilt houses and 60 families.

If you want to observe the lightning in Catatumbo, one of the best contacts is Alan Highton (alanbolt.com), a photographer, naturalist, and expert environmental guide from Venezuela who organises excursions on the lake to experience the lightning from a unique perspective.

HONDURAS

NICARAGUA

COSTA
RICA   PANAMA

Caribbean Sea

VENEZUELA

GUYANA

FRENCH
GUIANA

COLOMBIA

SURINAME

ECUADOR

Galapagos
(ECUADOR)

BRAZIL

PERU

La Rinconada ⊙

BOLIVIA

*Pacific
Ocean*

PARAGUAY

*Atlantic
Ocean*

CHILE

URUGUAY

ARGENTINA

Falkland Islands
(Islas Malvinas)
(U.K.)

N

South Georgia
(U.K.)

1 000 km

La Rinconada · Peru

The highest human settlement in the world is home to more than 60,000 people living at 5,100 metres in a severe climate

Sub-zero temperatures most of the year, relentless wind, lack of oxygen, landslides and bad roads, no sewage system and mercury pollution, all at an altitude of over 5,000 metres.

This may sound like a description of one of Dante's circles of Hell, but it is a settlement where more than 60,000 inhabitants live, driven to the slopes of the Ananea glacier, in the Peruvian Andes, by the 'thirst for gold' that began in the early 2000s and continues today.

La Rinconada is an urban agglomeration of makeshift buildings, built mainly between 2001 and 2010. During that time the price of gold rose by 230 per cent and thousands of poverty-stricken Peruvians saw in this mine – one of the largest in South America – an opportunity to make a fortune.

The mine is owned by the Peruvian state, which grants its exploitation to private companies. Miners work under a labour system called 'cachorreo' of 30 unpaid days with extraction tools provided by the contractors in exchange for three days of autonomous work with their own equipment, keeping any gold found during the three days. The illusion of being able to get rich during these 'interludes' of autonomy is enough to persuade many jobseekers to try their luck. Life for workers in the mining quarries at La Rinconada is among the hardest imaginable.

Mercury, used to split the gold from the rock in the extraction process, is widespread there and is highly toxic. On top of the difficulties of mining are the challenges of a hostile environment: at this altitude, exposure to UV rays is high and oxygen is rare.

Physiological and morphological adaptation, along with a greater capacity for oxygenation compared with natives of the lowlands, are essential to survive at La Rinconada. At an altitude of 5,000 metres, there is about half as much oxygen available as at sea level, since atmospheric pressure is about half as high. For this reason, Andeans, just like Himalayans, have better-developed lungs capable of extracting greater quantities of oxygen from the air.

La Rinconada is an extreme place in every respect. It is a haphazard collection of anonymous brick buildings and tin huts surrounded by endless piles of rubbish and no means of protection against the glacial cold. If the average daytime temperature stays just above zero, the temperature plummets sharply after sundown (as low as minus 15°C in July) and many workers shut themselves away in a bar or nightclub to consume alcohol. Prostitution, including child prostitution, is widespread in this hellish place.

The only comforts are electricity – brought in to ensure work can be carried out with machinery 24 hours a day – the internet, and many modern five-a-side football pitches. This might sound unusual considering the altitude, but it shows the ability of the inhabitants of La Rinconada to adapt to extreme conditions.

Those who, in spite of everything, would like to see this place at the edge of the world, can take a minibus from Putina and travel two and a half hours on a bumpy road, for a day trip with no overnight stay. There are no hotels – only windowless dive bars for passing miners.

The climate is divided into two seasons: a wetter, snowier and relatively milder one (temperatures around zero) from November to April, and a drier, colder one from May to October, with night-time temperatures often as low as -10°C and a marked temperature range between day and night.

© Marcin Osman / Shutterstock 1277781046

HONDURAS

Caribbean Sea

NICARAGUA

COSTA
RICA   PANAMA

VENEZUELA

GUYANA

FRENCH
GUIANA

COLOMBIA

SURINAME

ECUADOR

Galapagos
(ECUADOR)

PERU

BRAZIL

BOLIVIA

Arica

*Pacific
Ocean*

PARAGUAY

*Atlantic
Ocean*

CHILE

URUGUAY

ARGENTINA

Falkland Islands
(Islas Malvinas)
(U.K.)

South Georgia
(U.K.)

N

1 000 km

Arica · Chile

The seaside city where it never rains

Chile is a country of great climatic extremes. It is more than 4,000 km long and has the rainiest and driest places on the planet.

In the northern parts, on the border with Peru, lies Arica, the driest city in the world.

The data archive of the airport's meteorological station shows an annual average of just 0.8 mm – practically nothing.

The cold Humboldt marine current is responsible. It cancels out the evaporation of the ocean surface, blocking the upward motions responsible for the formation of clouds and precipitation.

Also known as the Peru Current, it is caused by the upwelling of deep and, therefore, very cold water, on the west coast of South America. It was described by the German naturalist Alexander von Humboldt in his work *Personal Narrative of a Journey to the Equinoctial Regions of the New Continent*, published in 1807.

To understand the phenomenon, it is first necessary to understand another ocean current – the Antarctic Circumpolar Current – which is triggered by the relentless westerly winds of the polar regions and pushes a constant flow of icy water toward Patagonia. As it approaches the South American continental margin, this mass of cold water is forced to rise to the surface and follow a diversion north for thousands of kilometres, lapping Chile's whole coastline.

It is the most important flow of cold water in the world, and has the most noticeable effects on climate. The portion of the Pacific Ocean crossed by the Humboldt Current is 8°C colder than other oceanic areas at the same latitude and has a major influence on the weather in the coastal areas of Chile, especially those north of Santiago.

Together with dry conditions, the Humboldt Current also causes the formation of coastal fog. During the winter (which in Arica is from June to September), the phenomenon known locally as 'camanchaca' may occur. This is when a bank of maritime clouds generated by the flow of warmer air from the Pacific flows over colder air crossed by the Humboldt Current. This thermal inversion can lead to the formation of haze banks and stratocumulus between the coast and the Andes.

The 'camanchaca' can generate cloudy days but is not capable of producing rain. However, its role within the desert climate of the Arica region is valuable: water, even drinking water, can be extracted from the fog. Chile started this practice in 1985, when the first 'fog catchers' were installed. These are polypropylene nets of a few square metres hung between two poles. Placed downwind, drops of water from the fog get stuck in the meshes and slowly slide into containers. One square metre of net can collect up to 14 litres of water in a day. The average is around 7 litres. The Catholic University of Santiago de Chile has set up a research centre on this technology, which has been

exported to Peru, Guatemala, the Dominican Republic, Nepal, Namibia and the Canary Islands. The water collected can be used for irrigation and personal hygiene, and it is quite simple to transform it into drinking water. Fog catchers are a good solution to contribute to the water supply of the smaller coastal municipalities in northern Chile, while in Arica most of the needs are supplied by aqueducts connected to the Rio Lluta and other rivers in the Andean highlands to the north-east of the city.

Arica, with a population of 200,000, is surprisingly temperate. Lying just north of the Tropic of Capricorn, cooled by the mitigating action of the ocean and thermal inversion breezes, it has a very pleasant temperature all year round, with highs reaching 27°C in February and lows of 14°C in July. The period when those occasional drops of rain can fall is limited to the summer season, which runs from December to February. This is why Arica is nicknamed the City of Eternal Spring. It is no wonder that the area was inhabited as far back as 10,000 years ago, as evidenced by many archaeological finds.

The Atacama Desert

The southern part of the Arica y Parinacota region borders the Atacama Desert, which is the driest coastal desert in the world, not counting the McMurdo Dry Valleys in Antarctica. The exceptional aridity – with an average of 0.6 mm per year of rainfall – is due to the Humboldt Current and to the geographical location of the desert, squeezed between the Chilean coastal mountain range and the Andes. The humid western currents from the Pacific are blocked by the Humboldt Current, while the north-east ones descending from the Bolivian Amazon are completely blocked by the Andes. In this impregnable, dry stronghold, rain is a mirage. According to the *New York Times Almanac*, no rainfall was recorded in some parts of the Atacama between 1570 and 1971.

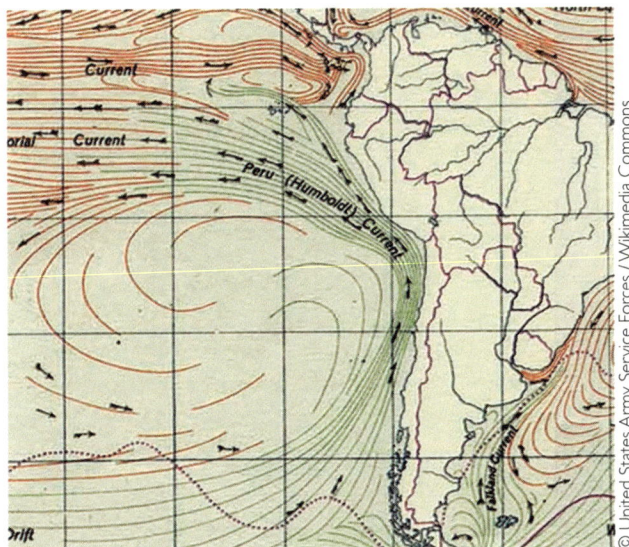

© United States Army Service Forces / Wikimedia Commons

HONDURAS

NICARAGUA

COSTA
RICA   PANAMA

Caribbean Sea

VENEZUELA

GUYANA

FRENCH
GUIANA

COLOMBIA

SURINAME

ECUADOR

Galapagos
(ECUADOR)

BRAZIL

PERU

*Pacific
Ocean*

BOLIVIA

PARAGUAY

*Atlantic
Ocean*

CHILE

URUGUAY

ARGENTINA

Falkland Islands
(Islas Malvinas)
(U.K.)

Bahía Felix

South Georgia
(U.K.)

N

1 000 km

The Bahía Félix lighthouse · Chile

The world record for rain in an inhabited place, with 325 days a year

The four Chilean naval officers who maintain the Bahía Félix (Felix Bay) lighthouse in Tierra del Fuego can count themselves among the few people who live in the wettest, and probably the windiest, place on Earth.

In this remote corner of Southern Chile, which comprises a myriad of small islands scattered in the Pacific Ocean at the western outlet of the Strait of Magellan, it rains (or snows) an average of 325 days a year.

The amounts measured by the rain gauge of the weather station are not excessive compared with other places on the planet, but the frequency of rainfall makes this one of the most extreme climates in the world.

There are several factors responsible for this weather pattern. First, Patagonia is the only landmass in the southern hemisphere (with the exception of Antarctica) beyond the 50th parallel south. There is no landmass whatsoever between the 56th and 60th parallel south. This means that the westerly ocean currents (SWW – Southern Westerly Wind) fed by the southern polar jet do not come across any obstacles as they circle the planet. They act as an endless generator of cloud ribbons that move rapidly over a vast, cold ocean. Southern Patagonia, and in particular the western side where the Felix Bay lighthouse is located, stands out against this flow as a powerless strip of land, continually slapped by wind and rain.

NUEVA DELHI
16.250 Kms.

SEUL
17.801 Kms.

SIDNEY
9.519 Kms.

ANTÁRTICA
3.838 Kms.

DUBAI
14.616 Kms.

USTED ESTA AQUÍ   You Are Here

In comparison, in the northern hemisphere, the higher percentage of dry land and the presence of warm sea currents means the jet stream has a more irregular pattern, with areas of semi-permanent low pressure created off Alaska, near Iceland and north-east Siberia. This results in a more complex alternation of high and low pressures and precipitation that, compared with the latitude of Chile's Tierra del Fuego (which is the same as Denmark), follows a less constant flow.

Summer at the Bahía Félix lighthouse runs from November to April and has temperatures between 10° and 2°C. In winter, from May to October, the temperature hovers around zero, with alternating rain and snow. The total annual precipitation is around 4,600 mm. Sunny breaks only last a few hours. Only in exceptional cases do lasting high pressures occur. In fact, since weather records started, the longest period with no rain was eight days.

The Bahía Félix lighthouse

The 14-metre-high lighthouse was inaugurated in 1907. Its function is to control navigation in the Strait of Magellan, a passage that has been strategic for the world's naval routes since its discovery by the Portuguese navigator in 1520. The construction of the lighthouse came after the 1881 treaty with Argentina, when Chile was given total control of the strait. After more than thirty accidents between 1869 and 1894, the majority with loss of ships, lives and precious cargo, the Chilean government decided to equip the southern coasts with an adequate signalling system operated and maintained by trained technical personnel.

The mission was entrusted to the Scottish engineer George Slight Marshall, who designed seventy lighthouses, one of which was on Felix Bay, which is considered strategically valuable. Today, the lighthouse has a radio station, a customs house, a dock and a repair room. Accessible only by helicopter, it belongs to the Chilean navy based in Punta Arenas.

ARGENTINA

CHILE

Drake
Passage

*Atlantic
Ocean*

*Weddell
Sea*

Neumayer Station

Maitri Station

Showa Station

Halley Station

Belgrano
Station

Mawson Station

*Indian
Ocean*

Zhongshan Station

ANTARCTICA

Amundsen Scott
South Pole Station

Vostok

Mirny Station

*Davis
Sea*

*Bellingshausen
Sea*

*Peter I
Island*

*Pacific
Ocean*

*Amundsen
Sea*

Casey Station

McMurdo
Station

Zucchelli
Station

Dumont d'Urville
Station

*Ross
Sea*

Antarctic Circle

*Dumont d'Urville
Sea*

N

1 000 km

Dry Valleys · Antarctic

The driest desert on the planet: where it never rains

The Dry Valleys are an anomaly in the Antarctic landscape. It is an area close to the Ross Sea, near the American McMurdo station, where rainfall is completely absent. This is a unique occurrence on the planet (even in the driest deserts such as the Atacama, the average rainfall is 1 mm per year).

As a result, the area strongly resembles Mars. Unsurprisingly, it is used as a base for testing equipment to be sent on expeditions to the Red Planet. Unlike the other Antarctic territories, the Dry Valleys are neither covered with ice nor snow, which is why they always appear dark brown on maps. How can this extreme climate and soil condition be explained?

First of all, the average precipitation in the whole of Antarctica is only 166 mm per year. This makes it possible to classify this continent as a desert (a place has a desert climate when precipitation is less than 250 mm per year). Within this already arid climate, the Antarctic Plateau and the Transantarctic Mountains play an important role. In inland areas, the air cools and increases in density when it comes into contact with the thick and extensive ice cap. As a result, it begins to slide toward the coast like a waterfall of air. During this process, just a few kilometres from the Ross Sea, the air mass encounters the Transatlantic Mountains (which are more than 4,500 metres high), and is forced to rise abruptly. It then crosses the ridges and descends toward the Dry Valleys at great speed. The wind that originates is called 'katabatic' or even 'drop wind', precisely because it is caused by masses of very cold air sliding down steep slopes. It can reach speeds of up to 300 km/h and its main characteristic is that it dries out the air, depriving it of all moisture. As if by magic, the Dry Valleys' katabatic wind makes clouds and snowflakes 'disappear'. Before they can settle on the ground, the wind causes them to sublimate, turning from tiny ice crystals into gas.

In these valleys, the wind is also responsible for curious sculptures, the so-called 'ventifacts', which are large rocks smoothed into singular shapes by the erosive action of sand particles raised by the currents. The presence of the wind and the absence of humidity do not even allow ice to form on the ground, and the valleys are eternally condemned to remain barren expanses of granite and limestone gravel. It is only during the short summer period that a few small lakes and a stream, the Onyx, appear, following the temporary melting of the surrounding glaciers.

The planet's deserts

An area is considered a desert when it experiences less than 250 mm of rain per year (in central Sahara, for example, the annual rainfall does not exceed 50–100 mm). Depending on the area's temperature, the deserts identified on the planet can be hot, cold, or polar. Hot deserts are found in subtropical and tropical regions. The main ones include the Sahara, the Namib, the Kalahari, Rub' al-Khali (Arabian Peninsula), the Atacama, the Syrian Desert, the Chihuahua Desert (Mexico and the US), Great Basin deserts (western USA) and the Great Australian Desert.

The cold deserts extend into the continental climate areas of the temperate belts and are characterised by marked temperature ranges, both daily and seasonally. The main ones are the Gobi Desert (- 40°C in winter and + 45°C in summer), the Karakum Desert in Turkmenistan and the Colorado Plateau in the US.

Greenland
(DENMARK)

Greenland
Sea

Arctic Circle

Jan Mayen
(NORWAY)

Norwegian
Sea

NORWAY

ICELAND

Hafnarfjall

Reykjavik

Faroe
(DENMARK)

Meridian of Greenwich

N

North
Sea

200 km

Atlantic Ocean

UNITED
KINGDOM

40°   30°   20°   10°   0°   10°

The Hafnarfjall weather station · Iceland

Fierce winds in Hafnarfjall

For Icelanders, 'good' weather essentially means no winds.

Rain, sub-zero temperatures, snowfall or fog are not a problem. But the presence or absence of wind determines how pleasant the day can be.

In Iceland, winds can blow at more than 200 km/h and play tricks on you. Those who are unfamiliar with the local climate should be very careful. It is not uncommon, for example, for the wind to rip car doors out of hands and severely damage them (tourists are advised to take out insurance against weather damage).

Given the country's location in the middle of the Atlantic Ocean, just below the Arctic Circle, no area is exempt from these climatic conditions. However, there are areas where gusts can take on hurricane-like characteristics. Atlantic cyclones move from west to east, and the deepest low pressures are often located south of Iceland. As a result, the most powerful winds are those with an east to south-east direction, drawn in by the low pressure moving east. The areas most exposed to these conditions are those on the south-west coast.

The Hafnarfjall weather station for example is located 40 km north of Reykjavik, at the foot of the Skarðsheiði mountain range. On 14 February 2020, gusts were recorded of 255 km/h coming from the east. The mountains behind the weather station contribute to increasing the speed, as the reliefs emphasise the sliding effect of the already impressive easterly winds (the phenomenon is called 'drainage wind' or 'katabatic wind').

The only human settlements on the stretch of road are a couple of hotels. There is no vegetation and no obstacles for the wind. If you find yourself travelling along this section of the Ring Road, make sure you check the weather forecast first. The official Icelandic meteorological office website is at vedur.is.

© NASA/GSFC, Jacques Descloitres / Wikimedia Commons

Pyramiden · Svalbard Islands, Norway

*The northernmost place in the world permanently inhabited
by at least 1,000 inhabitants*

Winter conditions in Pyramiden, a town in the Svalbard Islands, include snowstorms, temperatures that often fall below -20°C – with a record low of -46°C – raging winds, 250 days of snow cover a year, roaming polar bears, and the long polar night (the sun doesn't rise between late October and mid-February).

Pyramiden is the northernmost place in the world permanently inhabited by at least 1,000 people.

Located at 79°N latitude, the history of this last outpost before the North Pole is as unique as its weather.

At the end of the 1920s, after the Svalbard Treaty, the Russkij Grumant Russian mining company acquired the right to exploit coal deposits about 60 km north of Longyearbyen, the largest inhabited area of these Arctic islands. After the Germans destroyed the only base in existence there during the Second World War, mining activity was again in the hands of Soviet state-owned companies and resumed during the 1960s. As a result, a community of permanent residents began to grow there.

It was during these years that the settlement was renamed Pyramiden, after the pyramid shape of the peak behind the town, overlooking Adolfbukta Bay. The extreme climatic conditions did not deter the Soviet authorities, who created a miniature city with all the facilities needed for an 'ideal society'.

Between the 1960s and the 1980s, Pyramiden was home to more than 1,000 inhabitants. There was a kindergarten, primary school, swimming pool with heated seawater, hospital equipped for surgery, library with more than 50,000 books, a 300-seat cinema/theatre, gyms, a basketball court, and a five-a-side football pitch.

None of the houses in Pyramiden have kitchens; food is provided by a large, communal canteen.

The world's northernmost statue of Lenin was erected in the square of Pyramiden.

Besides the economic interest linked to mining, the reason for Pyramiden's existence is clear: the USSR wanted to demonstrate to the rest of the world its ability to make human life possible in the realm of polar bears, snowy blizzards, and ice.

Pyramiden's decline began in 1991 with the fall of the Soviet Union. The settlement was abandoned altogether in 1998, when the last 300 inhabitants were invited to find new accommodation.

Today, Pyramiden can be visited in the summer months with guided tours, and it is one of the most fascinating ghost towns on the planet. The freezing climate has helped preserve the buildings.

By land, Pyramiden can only be reached by snowmobile. It can also be reached with the 'Polar Charter' ship from Longyearbyen.

Hotel Tulpan, which was renovated in 2013 and is the only building with electricity, is stimulating renewed tourist interest in the area. Designed in a distinctive Soviet style, the hotel is open from March to October, and has a small museum and an excellent restaurant.

Today, six residents take turns keeping Pyramiden, the surreal and climatically hostile town at the edge of the world, alive.

Vannoya · Norway

Polar lows and mini Arctic cyclones

For as long as we can remember, sailors in Scandinavian countries have told tales of dangerous encounters with sudden but intense sea storms, known in meteorology as 'polar lows'. These are small but deep areas of low pressure that are difficult to predict, as they can form in just 24 to 36 hours and have diameters of only 100 to 300 km. Despite their small size, they are associated with extreme weather conditions.

In the presence of a polar low, changes in the weather can be sudden – blizzards emerge, roads and airports need to be closed, winds go from breezes to gales in less than 10 minutes, visibility drops, and rogue waves form at sea.

Due to its geographical position, Vannoya, an island on the Norwegian coast north of Tromsø beyond the polar circle (the 70th parallel north), is a place particularly exposed to the fury of this kind of storm.

In winter, the Gulf Stream warms the Norwegian Sea up to 30°C more than the areas furthest north (where the ice pack expands) and east (the continental areas of Scandinavia) which, in contrast, see temperatures plummet many degrees below zero. This difference results in the formation of two vast areas of very different pressures, making the European portion of the Atlantic Ocean in the latitude band between 50° and 70°N an area that is susceptible to the formation of winter mesoscale cyclones.

If icy currents from the pole cross this belt from October to April, the delicate thermodynamic equilibrium is broken, and the atmosphere undergoes a sudden upheaval. The more temperate and humid air is pushed up and, because of the contrast between the different physical variables, the flow of air triggers convective motions that form vertical clouds (cumulonimbuses) charged with energy. The low pressure that arises takes on the appearance of a small cyclone, where the temperature in the eye is less cold, similar to what happens in its better-known tropical relatives. In fact, the polar lows are also known as 'mini Arctic cyclones'.

While the north-west Norwegian coast is the most frequently affected area, this phenomenon also occurs in parts of Alaska and northern Japan.

The most intense part of the atmospheric phenomena associated with these depressions is discharged into the ocean and coastal areas. The energy produced is dissipated as the depression leaves the sea in the direction of the continent, where it loses the momentum required to continue growing.

Another reason Vannoya is a prime target for Arctic storms is its orography, i.e. the shape of the land.

The island covers an area of only 232 km2 but has two mountains, Vanniska and Peppertinden, whose peaks exceed 1,000 metres, if only slightly. But the steep slopes of the mountains accelerate the wind speed through the 'falling effect' (katabatic flows) and encourage more snowfall by acting as a barrage for the precipitation coming from the west and north-west. One of the worst Arctic storms in the recent past in Vannoya was in October 2001, when a polar low developed near the fishing village of Torsvåg in the north of the island. The gale capsized a boat, killing a crew member.

The origins and characteristics of this weather phenomenon remained largely a mystery until the late 1970s, when infrared satellites made it possible to identify these comma- or spiral-shaped mini cyclones.

The extreme hotel created by an Italian navigator

Inhabited by some 800 people, Vannoya is undoubtedly a place at the edge of the world. It is precisely because of its extreme characteristics that the Italian navigator and writer, Marco Rossi, decided to create the Nordlight, as a haven for travellers and readers. In the south-east of the island, on a 15-hectare plot with a 1 km-long beach and a lighthouse, he renovated two wooden buildings: the Red House and the House of Books. These residences, furnished with local materials, house maps and geographical atlases, and bedrooms designed with a particular attention to detail. A wood stove heats the common rooms and electricity is supplied by the nearby wind power plant. The large windows seem to have been made specifically to watch the gales and the northern lights. Rossi chose to stay in Vannoya after having spent his life as a sailor, navigating around the world. He loves the cold and the ocean and says: 'Nordlight is a refuge for travellers at the end of the world. Those who arrive can immerse themselves in reading and have the time to find themselves again.'

Fairbourne · Wales, Great Britain

Threatened by a 1-metre sea level rise, the seaside village will have to be 'decommissioned by 2045'

What could be extreme about the climate in a small Welsh coastal village, a destination for British pensioners and holidaymakers seeking tranquillity?

The answer lies in the effects of climate change and the resulting rise in sea levels threatening coastal resorts across the planet. In Fairbourne, this threat is having a tangible effect.

The first houses in the village were built in the 1920s close to the beach. The site was on a wide bay of alluvium just south of the Afon Mawddach, a large estuary where the rivers of Snowdonia, the highest area of Wales, converge. Fairbourne has not grown much (it has a population of just 700), but despite its size it has become a 'climate change case study'. A report by Gwynedd Council found that, by 2054, the area will no longer be habitable, and the village will have to be 'decommissioned by 2045'.

In the next 30 years it is predicted that sea levels could rise by 1 metre due to coastal erosion, increasingly violent storms, and global warming.

In the not-too-distant future, the rising sea level could be coupled with a flooding of the Afon Mawddach. Given that the Snowdonia highlands have an average rainfall of 3–4,000 mm per year, such an event is highly likely. In this case, no protection system would be able to save Fairbourne.

Residents are protesting: the warning caused the housing market to collapse, and no more mortgages are granted to buy or build new homes there. Many dispute the flood warning and refuse to be considered among the first potential climate refugees in Europe.

The Welsh public is asking that the Netherlands be taken as an example. For centuries the Netherlands has been doing its best to stem the tides – with remarkable results. However, in the face of climate change, the Dutch government has adopted a different approach since 2006, transforming farmland into flood plains and, in some cases, encouraging people to move elsewhere.

Natural Resources Wales, the local conservation organisation, says it is working on a solution to help communities like Fairbourne. Other towns and villages on this stretch of coast could also suffer from an uncertain future because of climate change.

The 'Bise' · Switzerland

The wind that causes Lake Geneva to freeze

Among the many winds that blow through the Swiss valleys there is one that is particularly violent. When it comes into contact with the waters of Lake Geneva it is capable of causing a curious, extreme phenomenon that freezes the surfaces exposed to the water spray.

The 'Bise', as this phenomenon is called, originates when an anticyclone between France and the UK meets low pressure in the Mediterranean.

Under these conditions, north-west Switzerland is squeezed between two opposing baric figures. On a weather map, this boundary line is marked by increasingly thick isobars, synonymous with gale-force winds.

The atmospheric dynamic created is similar to a river of cold, dry air that flows from continental Europe between the Jura Massif and the Savoy Alps, toward Lake Geneva.

As the valley narrows, the wind is further compressed in a sort of funnel effect, reaching speeds of over 100 km/h.

The Bise literally sweeps over the surface of the lake, causing waves more typical of a sea. In winter, this wind can cause the temperature to drop below freezing even during the day, and it is in these conditions that the south-west lakefront between Geneva and Versoix – the one most exposed to the wind – freezes in a spectacular way.

In February 2012, a Bise fuelled by Siberian air created a hibernation scenario on the lakeside in Versoix. The spray from the waves crashing on the parapets and the pier was carried dozens of metres further by the wind and froze instantly as soon as it hit the ground. Cars, lampposts, benches, and pavements were covered in a thick layer of ice that paralysed lakefront activities for several days at a time. Bise episodes occur every year on Lake Geneva, but the most intense ones that cause major ice formation, such as in 2012, are less frequent and tend to occur every seven years.

© Rijksmuseum / Wikimedia Commons

La Brévine · Switzerland

*A place of incredible thermal inversion: temperatures in the valley
can be 15°C lower than in neighbouring areas*

On 12 January 1987, the weather station at La Brévine in Switzerland recorded a near-unbelievable temperature of -41.8°C. If we consider only inhabited places, this is a record low on the Swiss territory. For La Brévine, it was also the start of a certain reputation.

La Brévine is in the canton of Neuchâtel, on the border with France. This area of great scenic beauty is part of the Jura mountain range. The village of La Brévine stretches on a plateau protected by mountains, at an altitude of 1,043 metres. The 600 or so inhabitants are all too familiar with the weather phenomenon that can bring about freezing winter nights. It is called thermal inversion.

Simply put, it's when temperatures are colder in the valley than in the mountains. It can occur anywhere on the planet, but is particularly impressive in La Brévine.

During the periods of high pressure that follow winter cold spells, frost settles in the low strata of this flat basin and forms a kind of buffer stuck to the ground. That's when terrain morphology and climate interact. On clear, dry nights, if the ground is covered in snow, the dispersion of heat accumulated during the day by the soil happens much faster. Normal irradiation is coupled with another phenomenon: as snow and crystals sublime in the dry air, it contributes to the dissipation of latent heat from the atmosphere. This is known as the 'albedo effect'.

With thermal inversion, the ground 'transfers' the cold to the layer of air in contact with it. But, a few tens of metres higher, the air column is not affected by this dynamic and cools down gradually, as it normally would.

Some business owners in the village of La Brévine, and even the municipality, have made the cold their symbol or, better yet, their trademark. For home furnishings, you can head to 'Meubles Alaska' (Alaska Furniture), for mountain sportswear there is 'Siberia Sports' and tourists can stay at the Auberge Le Loup Blanc, the 'Polar Wolf Inn'. For dinner, there's the L'Isba Restaurant, of course! The name refers to a traditional Russian countryside dwelling. Quite a few tourists go there to discover the 'Siberia of Switzerland'. Even in the middle of July, when daytime temperatures of 25°C are followed by crisp nights, the mercury can drop below 5°C. In times of global warming, it is a real blessing.

But climate change is also affecting La Brévine: winters with little snow are more frequent, and there were highs of 30°C for 15 consecutive days in 2019. If we use the heat record of 36°C in 2006, the maximum temperature variation in this corner of Switzerland is almost 78°C, one of the widest on the planet.

In the valley, temperatures can drop 15°C lower than in neighbouring areas. The minimum temperature is often lower in La Brévine

CZECH REPUBLIC

GERMANY

SLOVAKIA

AUSTRIA

HUNGARY

SWITZERLAND

SLOVENIA

Capanna Punta Penia

Milan

CROATIA

FRANCE

Venice

BOSNIA AND
HERZEGOVINA

SERBIA

ITALY

*Adriatic
Sea*

MONTENEGRO

Kosovo

Rome

Naples

ALBANIA

*Tyrrhenian
Sea*

GREE

ALGERIA

TUNISIA

*Mediterranean
Sea*

N

2000 Km

The Capanna Punta Penia mountain hut · Marmolada, Italy

A prime target for lightning – the sound of coursing electricity can be frightening

The Capanna Punta Penia mountain hut is on the summit of the Marmolada. At 3,343 metres, it is the highest point in the Dolomites. The hut was built at the end of the 1940s by the guide Giovanni Brunner, who adapted an existing Austrian military garrison from the First World War. The altitude makes this an extreme place from a meteorological point of view.

In winter, harsh weather and blizzards make the glacier inaccessible and, in summer, thunderstorms are violent, and the weather is characterised by gales and sudden snowfalls at night.

Carlo Budel, 49, is the manager of the Capanna Punta Penia and knows the climate well. Every June, he climbs the Marmolada to dig the hut structure out of the snow, heats it up and brings it back to life, ready to welcome the many hikers who climb to the summit in July and August.

In summer, inflows of cooler air at high altitudes sneak into the bubble of warm air stationed over central and southern Europe, and convective clouds blossom over the Alps with great speed, ready to pour their energy onto the rocky ridges.

The hut is a prime target for lightning, and anyone who finds themselves inside during a thunderstorm will not forget the deafening bursts.

There is no danger for the guests: the metal casing of the hut works like a Faraday cage, and the energy is discharged to the ground without affecting the people inside. But the sound of electricity coursing through – even more so if the bad weather arrives at night – can be frightening.

The 'Sentinel of the Dolomites', as Budel is nicknamed, embodies the ability of human beings to adapt to conditions that seem impossible. Budel was an assembly line worker for 20 years but saw the opportunity to run the refuge as a chance for rebirth and gave it all up to make a new life for himself at more than 3,000 metres up.

Apart from the thunderstorms, summer up there is an amazing season that offers indescribable sunrises and sunsets and the possibility, at times, of being above the clouds.

Unfortunately, global warming is hitting the Marmolada hard. On 3 July 2022, an 80-metre-high, 200-metre-wide serac broke away from the north face of the glacier, between Punta Penia and Punta Rocca, killing 11 people. Seven times during those days, the temperature at Punta Penia exceeded 10 degrees, with a peak of 13°C on 20 June (the average maximum in July is around 2–3°C).

A weather station was installed on 7 October 2022 at Punta Penia to monitor in real time. The readings can be viewed at www.marmoladameteo.it. The observatory became operational just in time to log a record temperature for the autumn period: an impressive +7.3°C on 29 October 2022.

Roccacaramanico · Abruzzo, Italy

The Italian village with the unofficial world record for daily snowfall

The mountains of Abruzzo, particularly those facing east like the Majella, can record huge snowfalls in winter. These snowfalls even compete with places in the Alps or Alaska and northern Japan for levels of snow accumulation.

The village of Roccacaramanico, in the municipality of Sant'Eufemia a Maiella, in the province of Pescara, is buried by snow almost every year.

At an altitude of 1,050 metres, it is officially inhabited by three people (the number rises slightly in summer).

The microclimate there is directly related to the way the mountain range is arranged around the settlement. The ridge of Mount Morrone (2,061 metres) to the west and the Majella group (2,795 metres) to the east form a wide valley, which comes together in a sort of funnel just behind Roccacaramanico. Opposite, on the north-east side and facing the Adriatic Sea, there are no obstacles, and the landscape slopes gently toward the coast.

In winter, this orographic gap becomes an ideal corridor for the icy Balkan winds. When there are cold-air incursions from eastern Europe, the north-east side draws moisture from the Adriatic and produces dense cloud bands that drift toward Roccacaramanico, which becomes the destination point for clouds and precipitation.

This kind of meteorological phenomenon, known as 'stau', works like a snow factory. In Roccacaramanico, it can snow for several days with astounding intensity. The town holds the unofficial world record for daily snowfall: on 17 December 1961, an accumulation of no less than 365 cm was recorded in 24 hours. The accumulation was recorded by the well-known Italian meteorologist, Edmondo Bernacca, but has not been confirmed by official bodies. The average snowfall in Roccacaramanico is around 3 metres per year, with a peak of 10 metres recorded in 1929.

Completely abandoned in the 1960s, the village is now experiencing a rebirth thanks to the Majella National Park and the presence of an ethnographic museum, some small accommodation facilities, and a tavern.

Fun fact: although the population decreased during the 1980s, one inhabitant remained in the village: Angiolina Del Papa. For years, he 'guarded' the village and worked as sacristan for the church.

Viganella · Piedmont, Italy

A mirror in the mountains to bring sunlight to a shady village
in the Western Alps from 11 November to 2 February

In the village of Viganella, in the Antrona valley of the Piedmont region, an eight-by-five-metre steel sheet has been installed. Made of glass and resin, and anchored to the ground at an altitude of 1,050 metres, its purpose is to reflect the sun's rays toward the small village left in the shade from 11 November to 2 February.

'Antro' in Italian means lair or den. As the word suggests, the valley is enclosed on both sides to such an extent that it resembles a deep, dark cave. This is a place where the light does not pass. It recalls the polar night of Arctic latitudes, but without the northern lights.

The village was first established in the 14th century, when coal merchants and miners, attracted by the iron deposits in the Ossola valley, began to settle in this remote corner of the Western Alps.

The village grew and sustained a glimmer of life throughout the Middle Ages. The advent of electricity brought new vitality. The 'climatic' turning point came in 1999 when the mayor, Franco Midali, informed Giacomo Bonzani, the gnomonist and architect in charge of the construction of the sundial on the parish church, that the winter dial would be, for obvious reasons, useless.

It was at that moment that the crazy idea was born: why not bring the sun onto the square artificially? The architect, a pure visionary, began work on the mirror project. It effectively saw the light of day, figuratively and literally, on 17 December 2006, when the contraption, measuring 40 square metres and weighing 11 quintals, was transported by helicopter and installed on the mountain behind the village.

From that day on, the little 'artificial sun' has been providing six hours a day of reflected light to the square in Viganella and its 200 inhabitants. Its operation is regulated by a computer: after sunset the mirror is repositioned based on the variations in the incidence of sunlight, so that the following morning it can resume its patient work of making winter feel lighter.

© Silvia Camporesi

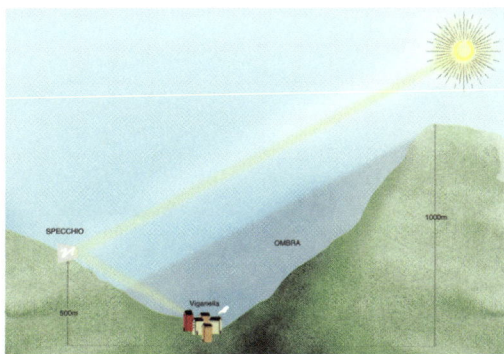

© Angela Larcher

Dallol · Ethiopia

The highest average annual temperature on Earth

Dallol, a former mining settlement within a volcanic crater system in Dancalia, north-east Ethiopia, is one of the few places in the world where the primordial energy that powers the Earth's core is still visible.

The average annual temperature is above 34°C – the highest on the planet.

The maximum temperatures are between 38°C and 45°C every month, while the minimums fluctuate between 30°C and 25°C.

Rainfall is rare.

The extreme climate, combined with geological conditions, have led to Dallol being nicknamed the 'Gateway to Hell'.

Dallol is in the Afar Triangle, a vast depression covered with crystallised salt after the withdrawal – some 20,000 years ago – of the Red Sea. Three continuously expanding tectonic plates meet under this deposit, which is the lowest point in Africa, creating a gigantic magma chamber, a genuine whirlpool of the Earth's mantle.

The lava flowing close to the surface gives rise to a geyser system and a network of concretions and crystals of potassium chlorides, sodium and magnesium. The phreatic eruptions of the main volcano, Erta Ale, form a landscape of spires immersed in the gases that settle on the acid ponds.

Mixed with sulphur, the salt from the depression creates crystalline formations with psychedelic hues.

In the local language, 'Dallol' means 'dissolved' and refers to the acid ponds that are often a death trap for animals and humans.

The heat of the ground combined with that of the air makes the plain surrounding the craters fiery. In this scorching bubble, the silhouettes of mud and twig huts appear to flicker like mirages. The huts are the dwellings of the Afar, who are nomads and the only people capable of surviving on this land.

The Afar are dedicated to the extraction and transport (by camel caravans) of salt, which to this day is their only source of trade and therefore of livelihood. In the moonscape of Dallol are traces of the mining activity of the last century, when the Italian company Co.min.a of the Montecatini Group dedicated itself to the extraction of potassium chloride, which was used to produce explosives, particularly during the First World War.

Today, the charm and astonishing colours of the hottest place in the world have attracted a certain type of tourism, and it is not uncommon to find queues of people walking up the slopes of Erta Ale. To get there, using specialised agencies is essential, and it is mandatory to be accompanied by an Afar guide and, given the political instability in the area, an armed policeman.

© Dimbak7 / Wikimedia Commons

Karthoum · Sudan

Haboob: the sandstorm engulfing Khartoum

It may look like an apocalyptic scene from a science fiction film, but it is actually a natural phenomenon common in many areas of the Sahel, the Middle East, Central Asia and Texas. Very large dust storms, which look like real walls of dust hundreds of metres high, with a front line as wide as 100 km, originate from strong thunderstorms and propagate at an average speed of 60 km/h over vast stretches of land.

One of the countries where this atmospheric phenomenon occurs the most, up to 24 times a year, is Sudan, and in particular the area around the capital, Khartoum. There, dust storms are known as 'Haboob' (from the Arabic 'Habb', meaning wind) and their formation follows a very precise pattern.

During the summer season, from April to October, the Inter-Tropical Convergence Zone (ITCZ) tends to shift north and the easterly trade winds start blowing toward Sudan from the highlands of Eritrea and Ethiopia. Thunderstorm areas develop in the mountains of these countries and are pushed west by the trade winds at high altitudes, losing moisture, and drawing strong north-easterly currents from the Bayuda Desert, which extends north of Khartoum. The turbulence generated by this mechanism results in a wind that lifts the grains of sand: the larger ones travel in contact with the ground, while the smaller ones are lifted into the air. In certain cases, the winds can form real walls of dust, giving rise to the characteristic red sky phenomenon. 'Haboob' refers to when visibility drops below 500 metres. At the peak of the storm, it is impossible to see more than a few metres ahead, and breathing becomes difficult.

Haboob episodes can be forecast by satellite observation and weather models, so that airports, roads, and schools can be closed in advance. If you are outdoors, it is advised to hold out for about 20 minutes, which is the time it takes for the initial wall of sand to pass (although the rest of the storm can last up to three hours) and breathe through a wet cloth.

© Akamoham / Wikimedia Commons

Kuwait City · Kuwait

The hottest temperature for an inhabited place

On 31 July 2012, the weather station in Kuwait City recorded a maximum temperature of 52.1°C, a record high for Kuwait City, the capital of Kuwait. Temperatures in June, July and August are prohibitive in this country bordering the waters of the Persian Gulf.

Kuwait holds the record for the highest temperature in an inhabited place, with 54°C recorded in Mitribah on 21 July 2016 (the world record belongs to Furnace Creek, Death Valley, California, with 56.7°C, but nobody lives there).

In Kuwait City, residents cope with the summer heat in the simplest way: by trying to avoid it. In these sweltering summer months, where even minimum temperatures often do not fall below 30°C, most Kuwaitis take refuge in air-conditioned offices and houses. They only go out to air-conditioned shopping malls in air-conditioned cars. In a city with virtually no shaded outdoor spaces, the shopping mall is the only public space where people can walk. Given Kuwait City is a very wealthy city – built on oil money – many can afford to avoid the heat. Unfortunately, not everyone. Some of the population, often migrant workers from South-East Asia, are forced to face it, risking their lives, or losing them.

The city's architecture contributes to the crazy summer temperatures. Concrete and asphalt cause temperatures to rise in the afternoon, when hard surfaces start to radiate back the heat they absorbed during the morning. Research by local architect Sharifa Alshalfan for the London School of Economics shows the city plans of Kuwait City were created in the 1950s by foreign architects with no experience or appreciation of the effects of climate. Kuwait City lacks green spaces, and there is a cultural aspect not conducive to proper urban planning: in people's minds, the outdoors does not exist, and a garden or courtyard is perceived as a waste of space. Also, the neighbourhoods are divided by highways, meaning residents are forced to use cars for even the most trivial errands.

© European Space Agency

Quriyat · Oman

The hottest night on Earth: 42.6°C in 2018

When people think of temperature records, they almost always refer to the hottest temperature reached in a day, or the coldest temperature at night or dawn. But have you ever wondered about the highest temperature recorded at night? In other words, what is the highest temperature recorded by a weather station from midnight on one day to midnight the next? The answer lies in the coastal town of Quriyat, Oman, where, during the night of 26 June 2018, the temperature did not fall below 42.6°C.

For the city's more than 60,000 inhabitants, or at least for those without air conditioning, this hellish interlude in the weather was destined to remain etched in their memories for a long time. After a maximum temperature of 49.8°C on 25 June, the temperature in Quriyat began to drop in the evening – but not at the usual rate. There was a high-pressure field on the Arabian Peninsula, which was pumping hot air from the hinterland toward the sea during the day. People expected temperatures to at least partially cool off, but the waters of the Gulf of Oman reached 32°C, with extremely high humidity affecting the entire coast south of the capital, Muscat, including Quriyat.

The land breeze – a light breeze created when the ground temperature becomes lower than the water temperature – was absent. The bubble of moisture created by the sea, like an invisible web of tiny vapour particles, prevented the dispersion of the heat that had accumulated during the day. When the atmospheric configuration started losing power, the data from the local weather station revealed the temperature remained above 41.9°C for no less than 51 consecutive hours, from 6 a.m. on 25 June to 9 a.m. on 27 June; an impressive figure even in a place accustomed to heat.

Moisture from the Indian Ocean, together with heat from the desert interior, make the summer climate on the coast of Oman extremely hot and sultry. Those wishing to visit Quriyat, a pleasant fishing town, should be aware that, between June and August, the average highs and lows are 40°C and 30°C respectively, with infernal nights always lurking.

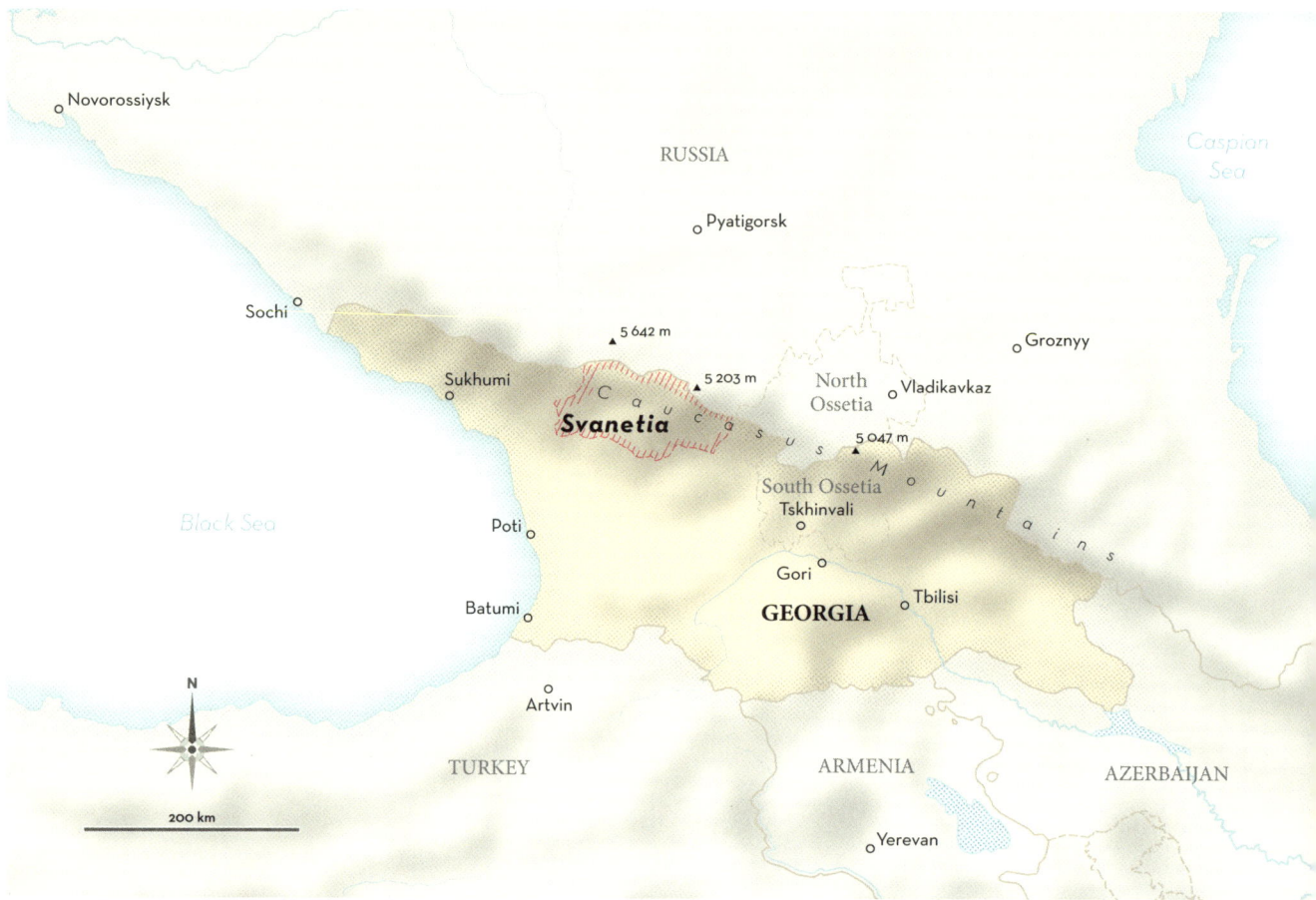

Svanetia · Georgia

Some 330 avalanches were recorded between 9 and 31 January 1987

Dotted with archaic villages and framed by superb snow-capped peaks, the region of Svanetia in Georgia is incredibly beautiful and untamed. It lies on the southern slope of the Great Caucasus, at the foot of Mount Shkhara which, at 5,193 metres, is the highest peak in Georgia.

The climatic characteristics of this area are the huge winter snowfalls caused by the interaction between the humid air from the nearby Black Sea and the harsh mountain temperatures. When the winds blow from the west-southwest, collecting moisture over the sea, the southern foothills of the Greater Caucasus act as a natural barrier for incoming clouds and snowfall concentrates, sometimes for weeks at a time, in the Mestia district.

In the winter of 1986–87, an unprecedented weather phenomenon hit the area. It snowed almost every day for 46 consecutive days. Above 2,500 metres, some 16 metres of snow fell, which was far too much to be retained by the steep, bare slopes (the limit of the forests is at 1,800 metres of altitude).

From 9 to 31 January 1987, some 330 avalanches were recorded. Mountain villages such as Chuberi, Ushguli, Mulakhi, Kala and Khaishi were heavily affected. In total, 105 people died and more than 2,000 houses were damaged. There are still ruins caused by the disastrous event.

Beyond this particularly tragic incident, avalanches abound during winters in the region. They are so frequent that a ritual is performed in local tradition, as testified to by the elders of the village of Ushguli: 'When an avalanche occurs on the slopes, we go to a forest downstream in that direction and a lamb is sacrificed to stop the mountain's intentions.'

Ushguli is considered the highest permanently inhabited place in Europe (it is situated at 2,200 metres and has about 200 inhabitants). During the three to four winter months, the road is cut off by the snow and the village is isolated from the rest of Georgia. It is essential for inhabitants to stock up on goods during the hot summer, and each family harvests potatoes, hay for the animals, and vegetables. They also stock up on flour, medicines, wood, canned goods, toiletries, and alcoholic drinks.

Locals feel a sense of powerlessness toward meteorological events and react with a mixture of acceptance, resignation, and resilience. These characteristics are so ingrained in the population that, after the 1987 tragedy, the place was not abandoned, and managed to recover. Thanks to the presence of some twenty-thousand-year-old defensive stone towers (the koshkebi), Ushguli was declared a UNESCO World Heritage Site in 1996, and today it has become a minor tourist destination that brings new economic opportunities.

Ushguli is set in the upper part of the Enguri Valley, below the glacier of Mount Shkhara. Despite the extreme climate, it remains one of the most fascinating places in Georgia and is the symbol of a land that has remained isolated and proud for millennia, even having its own language.

Aral Sea

Syr Darya

Lake Balkhash

KAZAKHSTAN

Almaty

Bishkek

Amu Darya

Shymkent

UZBEKISTAN

Ysyk-Köl

Tashkent

KYRGYZSTAN

Aydar Kul

Bukhara

Samarkand

Kashgar

TAJIKISTAN

Dushanbe

TURKMENISTAN

Bactria

Pamir

CHINA

Mary

Panj

Pamir

The Aral Sea ·
Uzbekistan/Kazakhstan

Toxic salt rains and the disappearance of the world's fourth largest lake

Human impact on the environment can create new and sometimes devastating weather events. This is what happened around the Aral Sea, between Kazakhstan and Uzbekistan. In recent years, the area has been subject to salt rains and sandstorms mixed with pesticides.

Satellite images testify to what is happening in this part of Asia. In the middle of the last century, the Aral Sea was the fourth largest lake in the world. Today, it is reduced to less than a tenth of its original size and has lost 95 per cent of its original volume.

In the 1960s, the USSR decided to increase its cotton production, and massive amounts of water were required.

The area surrounding the Aral Sea, and its two large tributary rivers – Syr-Darya and Amu-Darya – were identified as suitable for the cultivation of this 'white gold'. Even at the time, it was known the lake would lose much of its water because of this project, but the assumption was the lake would turn into a marshland, providing a new opportunity to cultivate rice.

Things did not go as planned: the supply system did not take into account the fragility of the land. From the outset, water wastage was enormous, and canals were built without any planning, causing the flow of the two tributary rivers to collapse. To make way for plantations, agricultural producer groups made extensive use of herbicides, which were later dumped in the rivers in the desert and scattered everywhere by the wind.

By 1987, the lake lost its river supply and much of its volume. It was divided into two basins, to the north and south. A few years later, the lake was further subdivided with the addition of eastern and western basins. As the lake retreated, it uncovered a vast plain littered with deposits of salt and toxic chemicals, what remained of weapons testing (the lake had also become a military testing area) and industrial projects, and the runoff of pesticides and fertilisers.

A new desert was born, named Akkum by the local people, i.e. White Sands. Supported by the World Bank, the Kazakh government took measures to stop desertification in the early 2000s. The construction of a dam allowed the rebirth of the Little Aral, the northernmost portion of the lake, where fishing resumed. Saxaul trees, a very hardy Central Asian native species capable of anchoring sand to the ground and limiting its dispersion, were planted in huge, arid areas. But the damaged territory is so vast that the road to improvement seems long and complicated. Meanwhile, extreme weather events continue to hit the region. When the constant east/south-east wind interacts with wetter air from the Caspian Sea region, clouds form and lead to salty, toxic rain which causes damage to crops and to the health of nearby people.

In May 2018, a sandstorm started on the shores of the lake. It was headed toward western Uzbekistan and northern Turkmenistan. Among the suspended particles were large quantities of salt and pesticide residues the wind had picked up in the Aral basin. The local population is particularly prone to respiratory and kidney diseases, and the mortality rate for children under the age of five in the area between Uzbekistan and Kazakhstan is second only to that of sub-Saharan Africa.

The local temperature has also changed – for the worse. Without the mitigating action of the lake's waters, winters have become colder and longer, summers hotter and drier, with an average temperature increase of between two and four degrees Celsius.

© NASA Earth Observatory

Barents
Sea

Novaya
Zemlya

Kara
Sea

Dickson o

RUSSIA

Yamal
Peninsula

Gyda
Peninsula

Doudinka o   o Norilsk

N

Vorkuta o

Novy Port o

Taz
Peninsula

Salekhard
o

Novy Urengoy o

Arctic Circle

200 km

Ob

Gulf of Ob

Taz

Yenisey

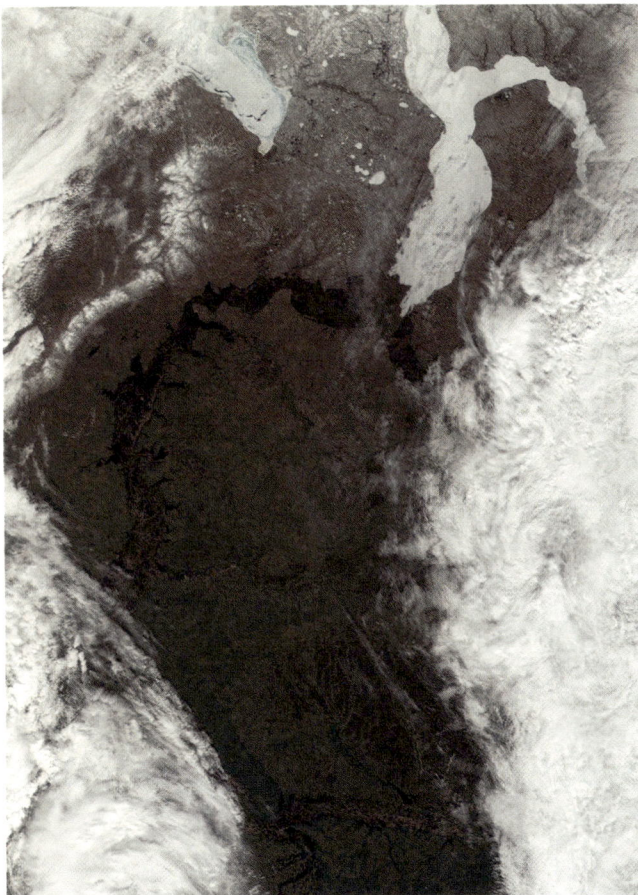

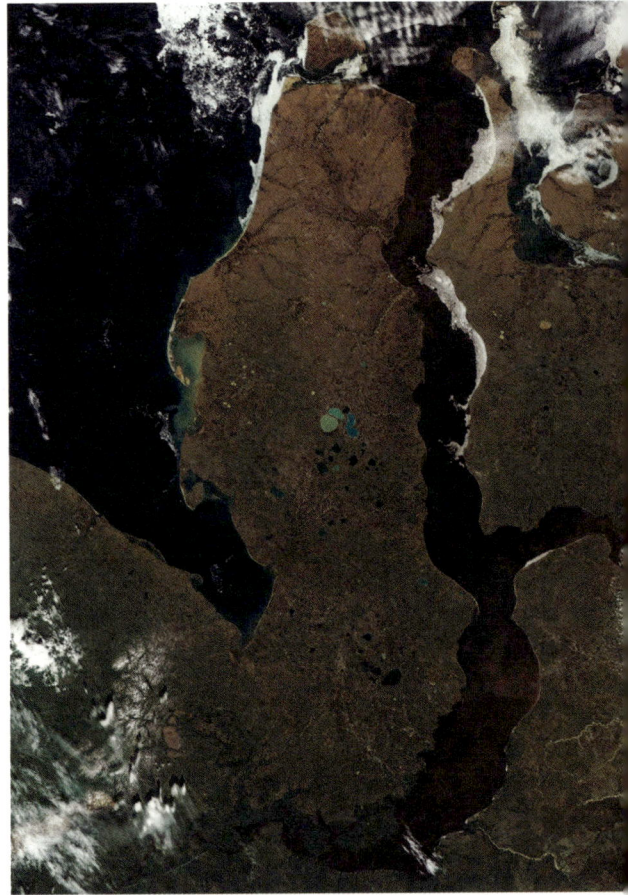

114

The Gulf of Ob · Siberia, Russia

When the weather is an artist

In early November 2016, some inhabitants of Nyda, in north-west Siberia, just above the Arctic Circle, witnessed an unusual scene. The beach near the town that lies on the shores of the Gulf of Ob was covered with a carpet of perfectly round balls of ice and snow.

Images went viral, prompting references to mysterious and supernatural phenomena.

Meteorologists were quick to give an explanation. Although rare, it has a scientific explanation and is linked to the rapid succession of specific weather conditions.

In the last days of October 2016, the Gulf of Ob, a large inlet where the river of the same name flows, began to freeze over in intense cold. It was coupled with heavy snowfall. The freezing process did not occur immediately and began to interact with the tidal cycle on the east coast of the gulf. As the water receded during low tide, ice crusts, snow and sand formed on the beach. At the same time, the area was hit by a windstorm that rolled the ice fragments onto the beach and shaped them with small sand grains into larger and larger shapes. With the return of the high tide, more water and ice were added, and the moulding continued. This alternating cycle ended up creating balls of different sizes. On those days, spheres as small as golf balls or even bigger than footballs could be found along the Siberian beach. Finally, a light snowfall covered everything, making the end result even more exquisite.

The uniqueness of the phenomenon is also due to the geographical configuration of the area: this very long inlet of the Kara Sea has an average depth of only 10–12 metres and freezes easily. Also, the fine, compact sand of the beach – without which the ice balls cannot form – is due to the sediments brought by the Ob River, one of the largest river systems in the world.

Norilsk · Siberia, Russia

Sub-zero temperatures and heavy pollution from nickel industries make Norilsk one of the most inhospitable places in the world, but 170,000 people live there

The Siberian city of Norilsk holds the record for being the city with the largest population north of the Arctic Circle. There are 170,000 inhabitants, many of whom are employed in the metallurgical sector; the city lies on the largest nickel and palladium deposit on the planet.

It is for this reason, and its remoteness, that a forced labour camp was established there during the Stalin era.

In the 1960s, after the closure of the gulag, architects designed what was to be an 'ideal city' conforming to Soviet socialist principles of work and society. The mines and mining facilities were expanded to make Norilsk the largest heavy metal mining complex in the world.

Buildings were arranged to reduce the impact of strong winter winds. The city grew without any green areas in a continuous succession of courtyards and very narrow walkways.

In Norilsk, there are about 130 days of snowstorms a year. Temperatures fluctuate between a maximum of -10°C and a minimum of -55°C and, for two months, the city is engulfed in polar night.

Yet, more than the climate, it is pollution that makes life in Norilsk difficult. Every year, almost 4 million tonnes of copper, lead, cadmium, nickel, arsenic, sulphur and other toxic chemicals are released into the air. Snow, which covers the ground for nine months of the year, sometimes turns red or yellow due to acid rain.

There is no vegetation within a 30 km radius, and the fruits the land produces in the short summer season are highly toxic. Life expectancy is 10 years lower than in other Russian cities, the risk of cancer is twice as high and respiratory diseases are very frequent.

So, why would anyone live in Norilsk? Many workers were encouraged to move there by the government during the Soviet period. The salaries offered were four times higher than in other regions of the country and, after 15 to 20 years of service, the government offered workers a flat.

Today, the families that grew up there enjoy the benefits of a self-sufficient system.

Jobs are secure and, although they are not as high as they once were, salaries are sufficient to cover any needs. Isolated from the rest of the world, anything the inhabitants buy here can only be spent in Norilsk, in an endless, closed circuit.

Proceeds from goods bought by citizens end up in the coffers of the mining companies that control the economy of Norilsk.

Norilsk Nickel, the largest mining firm, has pledged to move its plants out of the city and to control its emissions. In one of the most polluted places in the world, where even perennial wind and ice are a minor problem, this is perhaps the small hope that keeps families going.

Norilsk is a four-hour flight from Moscow, and few foreign tourists want to visit (according to the local Development Agency, around 200 tourists visit each year).

A visa is not enough. After deciphering the bureaucratic formalities on the website (available only in Russian) of the city administration, it is also necessary to obtain a special permit, or resort to a specialised tourist agency.

Russian photographer Elena Chernyshova is among the few people to document the harshness of the climate and life there. She lived in Norilsk for seven months in the winter of 2012–2013.

Ojmjakon · Siberia, Russia

The coldest inhabited place on Earth

The Earth has thousands of places that, from a climatic point of view, are inhospitable, yet humankind has managed to adapt and survive there despite adverse conditions. One of the most extreme places is undoubtedly Ojmjakon. In this small town of 800 inhabitants in the Republic of Sakha (Yakutia) in eastern Siberia, winters are so harsh that the town has been nicknamed 'the freezing city' and 'the pole of cold'.

The lowest temperature record there is -71.2 °C, in 1924. In Ojmjakon, winter lasts nine months and, between December and March, temperatures average between -30°C and -50°C. The cold is often accompanied by a phenomenon of freezing fog that covers every surface with ice.

Most of the inhabitants of Ojmjakon are descendants of the Turkic Yakut, hunters and reindeer herders native of north-east Siberia. Reindeer meat forms the basis of their diet, as agriculture is made impossible by permafrost (underground soil permanently remains below 0°C).

Fish also plays an important role, given the proximity of the Indigirka River, which does not fully freeze over thanks to the presence of thermal springs near its bed. The fish market is held in the open air, with produce obviously sold already frozen, although fresh. At the market, locals buy the ingredients they need to make stroganina: a dish popular with the people of Siberia, made of thin slices of frozen raw fish, served with salt and pepper. Other typical dishes include cubes of frozen horse blood with macaroni and frozen raw horse liver.

A typical house in Ojmjakon is made of wood and heated with coal. Toilets are in small, unheated huts in the garden to avoid the problem of pipes freezing. For the same reason, it is important not to turn off the engine of a parked car.

There is only one shop in the village, which supplies the inhabitants with everyday essentials. Outdoor walks during winter are generally quick: at -45°C, the skin freezes in five to ten minutes. That said, the inhabitants of Ojmjakon lead a life they feel is quite normal. They have simply learnt to adapt, and the so-called Russki chai – Russian tea, as they affectionately call vodka – surely helps.

Ojmjakon may have the same latitude as southern Iceland, or central Norway (it lies on the 63rd parallel north), but its climate is quite different. In contrast, there are no western Atlantic currents to mitigate the weather and the continental climate suffers from a phenomenon of frost accumulation typical of the Siberian–Russian plains. Thermal inversion, the albedo effect, and poor insolation all mean the cold is self-generating. These factors cause temperatures to plummet to incredible levels. While the cold in winter is extreme, it is common to also experience a few days of heat during the short summer, with temperatures reaching up to 30°C. With the warmer temperatures, nature goes into full bloom, including the rapid reproduction of mosquitoes. If you are planning a trip there, you should know there are no hotels, but you can stay with the locals. Adventurous, cold-weather tourists should therefore contact local agencies.

Hovd · Mongolia

After a hot, dry summer and a particularly harsh, snowy winter,
a dzud is a harbinger of hunger, death and migration

With more than 250 days of sunshine a year, Mongolia is known as the 'Land of the Blue Sky' – a definition that could be misleading when it comes to the harsh climate of this land. During the winter, temperatures drop to -50°C, and living conditions can become unbearable for the country's many semi-nomadic herders.

Conditions are particularly harsh when a cold and snowy winter follows a hot and dry summer. This is when what the Mongols call 'dzud' occurs. During dzud the animals, weakened by insufficient summer fodder and small fat reserves, cannot find food in the snow-covered ground and die of cold and starvation.

In a country with 3 million inhabitants, 70 million cattle, and 300,000 people living off pastoralism, dzud is synonymous with death, hunger and migration.

This weather phenomenon is part of Mongolia's climatic history, and herders have always taken into account the possibility of losing part of their livestock every year. However, over the past two centuries, the frequency of dzud has increased by up to five times. During the 19th and 20th centuries, the combination of a dry summer and a particularly cold and snowy winter occurred about once every five to seven years in Mongolia, but in the 2000s it averaged once every two to three years. Mongolia was hit by three dzud in a row between 1999 and 2002, and more than 12,000 herder families lost entire herds.

Among the hardest-hit areas were the western provinces of Gov'-Altaj and Hovd. In the latter, the catastrophic dzud of 2010 wiped out 11 million sheep, cashmere goats, cattle, and horses – more than 20 per cent of the country's total. In late 2022, a report by the United Nations Office for the Coordination of Humanitarian Affairs (OCHA) on data from the Mongolia National Agency for Meteorology and Environmental Monitoring (NEMHEM) warned of a severe dzud during the cold and snowy winter of 2023 in Hovd Province and the rest of Western Mongolia.

As expected, in January 2023 temperatures dropped to -50°C in the provinces of Hovd and Zavkhan, and snowfall reached 37 cm, against the average of 24 cm. Livestock losses were, again, very high.

The increased frequency of this phenomenon can be attributed to climate change-induced seasonal extremes: dry and hot summers have become more frequent, while in winter, greater humidity in the atmosphere has increased the extent of snowfall in semi-desert and steppe areas, just like the one in Hovd. The increased frequency of dzud does not give many herders time to reorganise their herds, and thousands are forced to abandon their activity and land and move to the capital, Ulaanbaatar, to seek work.

The percentage of Mongolians living in urban areas rose from 53 per cent in 1995 to 68 per cent in 2018. In ten years, from 2008 to 2018, Ulaanbaatar has grown from 1 to 1.5 million inhabitants. This growth is reflected in the urbanisation: entire districts of ger (Mongolian yurts) and endless stretches of hastily built tents, poorly connected to urban services and infrastructure, have sprung up in the capital's suburbs.

© tashinamgyal / Pixabay

MONGOLIA

KAZAKHSTAN

UZBEKISTAN

TURKMENISTAN

KYRGYZSTAN

TAJIKISTAN

CHINA

AFGHANISTAN

IRAN

PAKISTAN

o Srinagar

Chandigarh
o

NEPAL

BHUTAN

Guwahati
o

Brahmaputra

New Delhi ■

Jodhpur
o
Jaipur
o
Agra
o

Ganges

Lucknow
o

Patna
o

Meghalaya

Yamuna

Varanasi
o

MYANMAR

Tropic of Cancer

Ahmedabad
o

Jabalpur
o

Narmada

Ranchi
o

Kolkata
(Calcutta)
o

Mahanadi

INDIA

Arabian
Sea

Mumbai
(Bombay)
o

Godavari

Hyderabad
o

Vishakhapatnam
o

Bay
of Bengale

Krishna

Panaji
o

Bangalore
o

Chennai
o

Coromandel Coast

Andaman
and Nicobar
(INDIA)

Mamgalore
o

Kaveri

Mysore
o

Malabar Coast

Madurai
o

Lakshadweep
(INDIA)

Kochi
o

Laccadive
Sea

SRI LANKA

MALDIVES

N

Indian
Ocean

Equator

1 000 km

Meghalaya · India

The rainiest place on Earth

The state of Meghalaya is a mainly mountainous strip of land about 300 km long and 100 km wide, at its widest. It is in north-east India and has a planetary record of 12 metres of rain on average each year.

Meghalaya literally means 'abode of clouds' in Sanskrit. It doesn't rain all day, but it rains almost every day.

Naturally, intense rainfall also occurs at the equator, but here it is the monsoon, which is most intense between June and September, that raises the average annual rainfall.

The cause of this extreme climate is related to the general shape of the land. Hot and humid currents funnel through from the Bay of Bengal to the plains of Bangladesh until they collide with the mountain range that forms the Shillong Plateau, rising as high as 3,000 metres. The Bangladesh plain acts as a launch pad for the rainfall. A buildup on the southern slope of the plateau only reinforces the rainfall.

This is precisely also where the two main population centres of this area are located, namely Cherrapunjee and Mawsynram. At an altitude of 1,400 metres, the two towns have populations of 15,000 and 2,600 respectively and compete for the record of the rainiest town in the world.

Life in the two towns is punctuated by cloudbursts, floods, and fog. The market is held twice a week even in the worst weather and students go to school in their uniforms regardless of the downpours. Along the streets, workers can be seen working under the shelter of traditional Khasi umbrellas, known as 'knups'. Made of bamboo and banana leaves, these umbrellas sit atop their heads and offer a solution to keep their hands free, enabling them to continue working while the rain rages.

© Amos Chapple Photography

The economy is based on agriculture (potatoes, rice, maize, pineapples, and bananas are grown), clandestine mining, and a bit of tourism.

Meghalaya has two national parks and three nature reserves. Mountaineering, climbing, trekking, hiking and water sports are practised there.

For those who want to discover this corner of the planet where nature is magical and the atmosphere is drenched in mysticism, it is just a matter of picking dates when it is likely to rain less, and choosing when the temperatures will be better. From March to May the temperature is better than at any other time of the year (around 20°C). During the monsoon, from June to September, temperatures drop. It is cooler in the winter (averaging around 10°C), from October to February, and while rain persists, it is less intense. This is when the landscapes are at their most impressive, thanks to the presence of rushing waterfalls, which can be reached along the magnificent natural root bridges crossing the Khasi river valleys.

In this extremely rainy climate, humankind has managed to harness the roots of rubber trees to build 'living bridges', which are a sight definitely worth admiring.

One day of rain in Cherrapunjee: more than twice what falls in London in a year

According to data from the India Meteorological Department, the maximum amount of rain that fell in 24 hours was in Cherrapunjee. An incredible 1,560 mm fell in a single day on 16 June 1995. That's more than twice what falls in London in a year.

© Amos Chapple Photography

KAZAKHSTAN

MONGOLIA

UZBEKISTAN

KYRGYZSTAN

TURKMENISTAN

TAJIKISTAN

CHINA

IRAN

AFGHANISTAN

o Srinagar

Komic O

PAKISTAN

Chandigarh o

BHUTAN

New Delhi ■

NEPAL

Guwahati o

Brahmaputra

Jodhpur o   Agra o   o Lucknow

Jaipur o   *Ganges*   Patna o

Yamuna   Varanasi o

Tropic of Cancer

Ranchi o

*Arabian
Sea*

Ahmedabad o   Jabalpur o

Kolkata
(Calcutta) o

MYANMAR

Narmada

Mahanadi

INDIA

Mumbai o
(Bombay)

Godavari

Hyderabad o

Vishakhapatnam o

*Bay
of Bengale*

Krishna

Panaji o

Coromandel Coast

Mamgalore o

Bangalore o   o Chennai

Kaveri

Mysore o

**Andaman
and Nicobar
(INDIA)**

**Lakshadweep
(INDIA)**

Malabar Coast

Kochi o   Madurai o

*Laccadive
Sea*

SRI LANKA

MALDIVES

N

*Indian
Ocean*

Equator

1 000 km

Komic · India

The highest inhabited place in the world accessible by car,
with a difficult climate for the inhabitants

As the sign at the entrance of the village of Komic says, this is 'the highest inhabited place in the world accessible by car'. Located at an altitude of 4,587 metres in the Spiti valley on the Indian side of the Himalayas, the settlement was established in a natural, bowl-shaped basin, surrounded by bare mountains more than 6,000 metres high. When added together, the harsh climate, high altitude, lack of communication and poor soil fertility make life there extremely hard. The biggest problem, apart from the cold, is how dry the land is.

In the spring, the water generated by the thaw tends to rush down the sides of the mountains, feeding the Spiti River, while the soil at Komic only retains a smaller percentage of it. With climate change, this has worsened: according to research by Jawaharlal Nehru University in Delhi, annual temperatures in the Indian Himalayas have increased by up to 2 degrees in 20 years, while glaciers have shrunk by 13 per cent in the last 50 years.

There is less ice and snow in winter, and less water in summer, because Komic is in a rainfall shadow region in relation to the monsoon and, from May to October, rarely benefits from rain. After the dry and sunny months of May and June (the best months to visit the area), and a cloudier but still dry and mild period from July to October, the extreme weather arrives in November, when temperatures plummet and it snows heavily.

At night, it reaches -30°C. At that point, and until April, the road from Manali to Kaza, along the Spiti River, is closed due to avalanche hazards, and Komic and its 114 inhabitants remain cut off from the rest of the world.

Who are these high-altitude heroes? A large part of the population is made up of Buddhist monks of the Tangyud Monastery, but there are also families of shepherds and, in recent years, some people who have started to offer tourist services. There are in fact two guesthouses, a restaurant, and a taxi-bus agency in Komic.

Komic's climate is not suited to agriculture, and the only agricultural activity is the rearing of sheep, horses, and yaks. Tourists will have to consider that even just a short walk can cause fatigue due, in part, to the lack of oxygen at such a high altitude. Between the seasonal and diurnal temperature ranges and the erosive action of the ice that alternates with the relentless high-mountain sun, the terrain is reduced to a kind of dust that quickly blows away in the wind.

HIMACHAL PRADESH PUBLIC WORKS DEPTT.
DIVISION — KAZA
HIGHEST VILLAGE IN WORLD
CONNECTED WITH MOTORABLE ROAD
VILLAGE — KOMIC
POPULATION — 114 CAPITA
ALTITUDE — 4587mtr.

SPITI 2018

KAZAKHSTAN

MONGOLIA

UZBEKISTAN

TURKMENISTAN

KYRGYZSTAN

TAJIKISTAN

IRAN

AFGHANISTAN

CHINA

PAKISTAN

o Srinagar

Chandigarh
o

New Delhi ■

NEPAL

BHUTAN

Brahmaputra

Guwahati
o

Jodhpur
o

Jaipur
o

Agra
o

Ganges

Lucknow
o

Yamuna

Varanasi
o

Patna
o

Ranchi
o

Kolkata
(Calcutta)
o

MYANMAR

Tropic of Cancer

*Arabian
Sea*

**Rann
of Kutch**

Ahmedabad
o

Jabalpur
o

Narmada

Mahanadi

INDIA

Mumbai
(Bombay) o

Godavari

Hyderabad
o

Vishakhapatnam
o

*Bay
of Bengale*

Krishna

Panaji
o

Coromandel Coast

Bangalore
o

Chennai
o

Mamgalore o

Kaveri

Mysore
o

**Andaman
and Nicobar
(INDIA)**

**Lakshadweep
(INDIA)**

Kochi
o

Madurai
o

Malabar Coast

*Laccadive
Sea*

SRI LANKA

MALDIVES

*Indian
Ocean*

N

Equator

1 000 km

The Great Rann of Kutch · Gujarat, India

Blinding heat from the reflection of the sun and light on the white soil

In the state of Gujarat, the westernmost state of India, on the border with Pakistan, lies the Rann of Kutch, a gigantic brackish marsh that used to be fed by the Arabian Sea until tectonic movements raised the seabed.

The Rann of Kutch is marked by extreme temperatures, from peak heats between May and June (records reaching nearly 50°C) to monsoon rains from late June to September.

During the short, wet season, the swamp floods and the salt expanse becomes a gigantic lake.

At the end of September, the water evaporates, leaving behind only the salt in which the ground is drenched, and everything turns into a great white expanse. The landscape takes on a lunar appearance: endless salt expanses stretch as far as the eye can see, shrouding everything in a blinding white blanket.

As early as February, maximum temperatures can exceed 30°C, and in April it can easily reach 40°C. May is the month where the heat is the fiercest, with peaks of 48–49°C. Few people manage to work in salt mining during this period: between the relentless rays of the sun and the light reflected from the white soil, working in those conditions is unbearable. This is why families from the salt-mining villages that have sprung up in the surrounding area to exploit this resource travel to the swamp as early as October, to take advantage of the more bearable temperatures for as long as possible. They move with their tents near the swamp and stay there for at least six months. Only a few are able to walk barefoot over entire expanses of muddy swamp in the less exploited areas on the edge of the most profitable salt pans.

Over the six months, an entire family will earn less than 200 euros working the salt marshes. They will have to survive with those earnings for the entire year.

With the Salar de Uyuni in Bolivia, this is one of the world's largest salt deserts

The Rann of Kutch is one of the world's largest salt deserts, but unlike others, such as the Salar de Uyuni in Bolivia, it has not yet fallen into the hands of tourists and offers the chance to observe at first hand how local communities, such as the Agariya, have adapted to this extreme climate and environment to make a living from it.

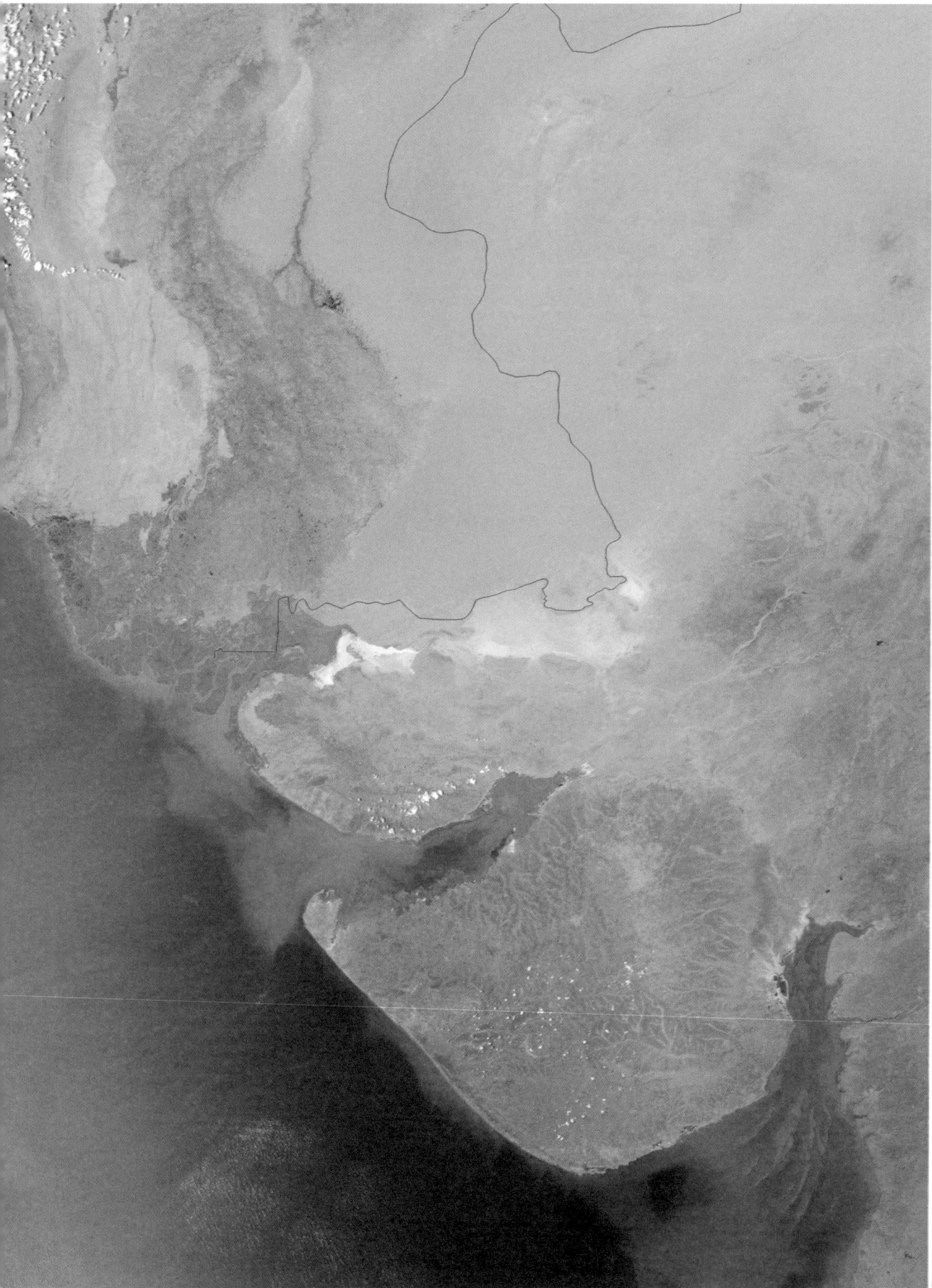

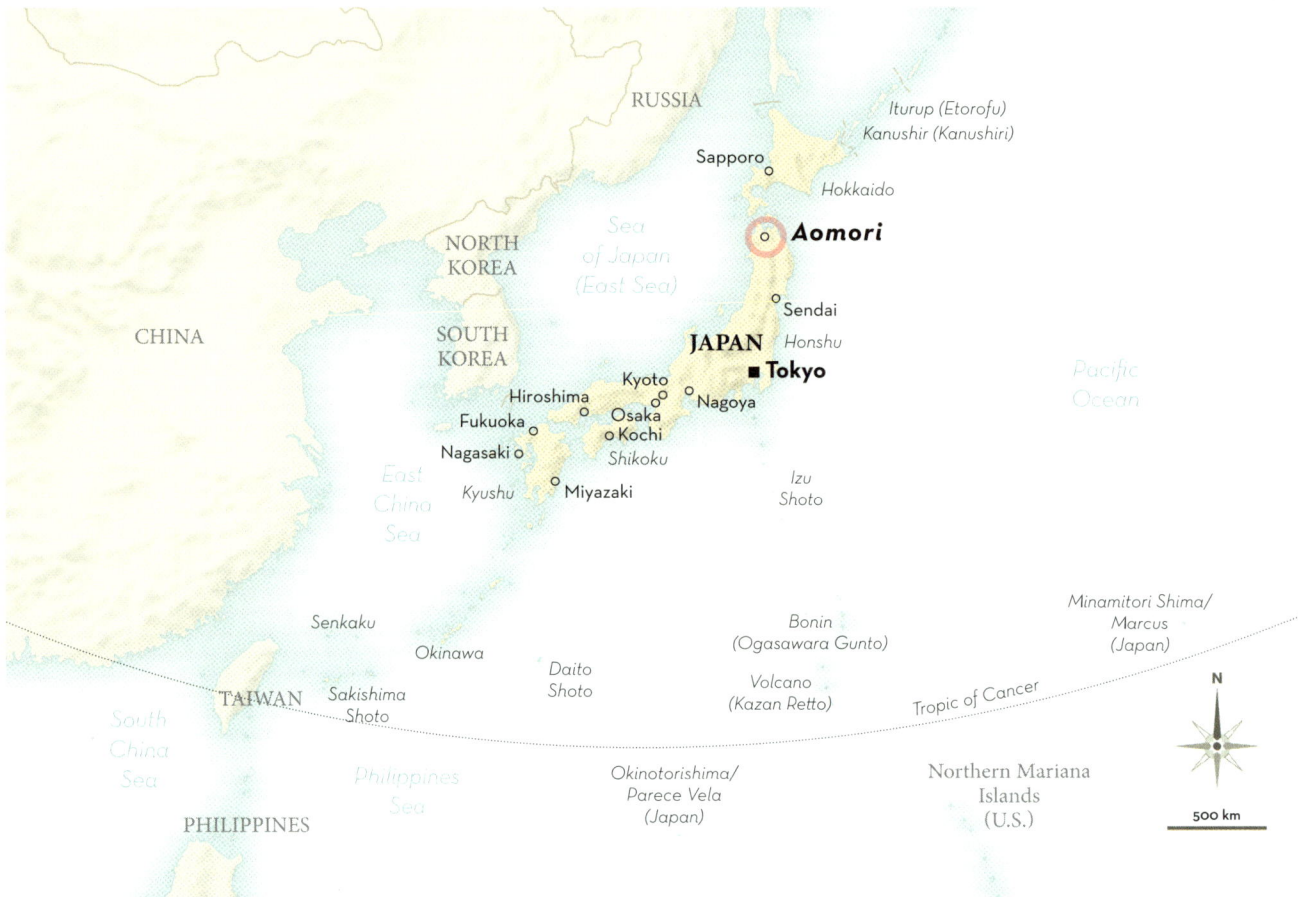

RUSSIA

Iturup (Etorofu)
Kanushir (Kanushiri)

Sapporo

Hokkaido

Aomori

NORTH
KOREA

Sea
of Japan
(East Sea)

Sendai

CHINA

SOUTH
KOREA

JAPAN   Honshu

Kyoto   ■ **Tokyo**

Hiroshima   Nagoya

Fukuoka   Osaka
Kochi

Nagasaki   Shikoku

Kyushu   Miyazaki   Izu
Shoto

East
China
Sea

Senkaku   Bonin
(Ogasawara Gunto)   Minamitori Shima/
Marcus
(Japan)

Okinawa   Daito
Shoto   Volcano
(Kazan Retto)   Tropic of Cancer

TAIWAN   Sakishima
Shoto

South
China
Sea   N

Philippines
Sea   Okinotorishima/
Parece Vela
(Japan)   Northern Mariana
Islands
(U.S.)

PHILIPPINES   500 km

Aomori · Japan

The place, at the same latitude as Rome, that receives the most snow

If you exclude the mountains, what are the places on Earth that receive the most snow during the winter? The gold medal goes to the Japanese city of Aomori. Located in the north of the island of Honshu, Aomori is home to 300,000 people.

Every year, an average of almost 7 metres of snow falls from November to March. Incredible? Yes, especially if you consider that Aomori is by the sea and at the same latitude as Rome.

So why do such large amounts of snow fall there? Only 300 km from Aomori as the crow flies, on the opposite shore, is Russia's Vladivostok, the gateway to the vast, frozen lands of Siberia. When the winds in winter come from the north-west, particularly cold air is sucked out of the Russian continent toward the coast. Unhindered, the frost crosses the Sea of Japan and Mutsu Bay. This is how the atmospheric phenomenon of sea-effect snow forms. It occurs when particularly icy, dry air flows over a humid mass (sea or lake), raising water vapour that condenses into long, narrow cloud bands. Like snow trains, these cloud bands roll directly toward the northern Japanese coast.

Average winter temperatures in Aomori range between -3°C and +2°C. The record amount of snow that fell in a single winter was 12 metres, in 1986.

A similar phenomenon occurs in certain cities on the shores of the American Great Lakes, such as Buffalo or Syracuse. There, it is known as 'lake-effect snow'.

© NASA Visible Earth

CHINA

TAIWAN

Hong Kong

Batan
Islands

Babuyan
Islands

Pacific
Ocean

Laoag

South China
Sea

Baguio

Dagupan

Luzon

Philippines
Sea

■ **Manila**

Batangas

Naga

Mindoro

PHILIPPINES

Calbayog

Samar

Roxas

◎ **Tacloban**

Panay

Leyte

Iloilo

Cebu

Palawan

Puerto Princesa

Negros

Bohol
Sea

Butuan

Sulu
Sea

Pagadian

Mindanao

Cagayan
Sulu

Davao

Zamboanga

Moro
Gulf

General
Santos

Basilan

Jolo

Tawi
Tawi

MALAYSIA

BRUNEI

Borneo

Celebes
Sea

N

INDONESIA

500 km

Tacloban · The Philippines

The place most exposed to the passage of tropical cyclones

Tropical cyclones represent the extreme atmospheric phenomenon par excellence. Their power, size, spread, and destruction in terms of human losses and economic damage make them the most monitored and studied meteorological phenomenon on a planetary level. They have different names depending on the geographical area in which they originate: 'typhoons' in the North Pacific and Japan, 'cyclones' in the Indian Ocean, 'willy-willy' in Australia, 'hurricanes' in the Caribbean and the rest of the world.

The worst affected country in the world is the Philippines, where on average as many as nine typhoons pass through each year. In a country of 96 million inhabitants with one of the lowest GDPs in the world, a fragile infrastructure, and more than 7,000 islands, typhoons can be catastrophic. Among the worst in memory, Typhoon Yolanda killed 8,000 people and displaced 4 million, wiping out several population centres, including the city of Tacloban in Leyte province in early November 2013.

Originating in the warm waters of the western Pacific at the height of Micronesia, Yolanda swept through the central Philippines with winds of 230 km/h and a maximum gust of 314 km/h. The 'storm surge' – a storm wave associated with the passage of every tropical cyclone – destroyed Tacloban, which overlooks San Pablo Bay, at the end of a shallow, slightly sloping inlet. Yolanda's 260 km/h winds hit the coast perpendicularly, and in their swirling motion raised a wall of water that grew even more when it was forced inside the bay, flooding everything for hundreds of metres and damaging 90 per cent of the structures. One of the most iconic images of this extreme phenomenon is the shipwreck that ended up in the ruins of a residential area north-west of the harbour. The bow of the MV *Eva Jocelyn* was later turned into a memorial and became a tourist destination, demonstrating the resilience of the Filipino people, who have long been battered by weather events but are always able to rise again.

After the typhoon of 2013, the government revised its urban development plans by launching the Tacloban North project, to relocate the population to safer areas north of the coastal zone. However, due to delays in its implementation, many families were forced to return to their makeshift homes in completely vulnerable coastal neighbourhoods. Despite the difficulties, Tacloban is now one of the fastest growing cities in the Philippines. Banks, retail outlets, hotels and restaurants have reopened, new businesses are appearing, and tourism is gaining a foothold again. In 2014, journalist and TV producer Francesco Conte travelled to the Philippines to make a documentary about the consequences of typhoons and the dangers of climate change. Available on Vimeo, *Stormed* is an interesting film for anyone who is keen to learn more about the subject.

Tropical cyclones

Tropical cyclones originate at sea with temperatures no lower than 27°C and in the area on earth where trade winds converge. These areas are known as the 'Inter-Tropical Convergence Zone' (ITCZ). This belt encompasses the planet's oceans and, depending on the time of year, moves between the equator and the tropics. In the ITCZ, the air is very unstable and full of convective motions that give rise to thunderstorms and storms. The 'Coriolis force', which is the deflection of atmospheric winds caused by the earth's rotational motion, also has a role to play in these already turbulent conditions. The Coriolis force is zero at the equator but, at a distance of at least 500 km from it, it can cause deviations of the converging air. As a result, the air begins to move in a circle, with increasingly higher speeds as it approaches the centre of the vortex (this is why tropical cyclones never form at the equator, but just above or below its line).

If all the pieces of this complex mechanism fall into place, a normal tropical storm within the ITCZ can trigger a growing suction of energy and steam to the point where it turns into a vortex. The eye of a cyclone within the ITCZ can reach about 25 km in diameter, with average winds of more than 119 km/h blowing around it. In fact, it is beyond this threshold that storms become hurricanes. The power of a hurricane is classified in five categories by the Saffir-Simpson scale (a cyclone on scale 5 has average winds exceeding 250 km/h).

The entire cloud system rotates around the eye. This wall of clouds can reach up to 15 km in height and between 300 and 800 km in diameter. Once formed - there are between 50 and 60 cyclones recorded worldwide each year – cyclones begin their journey, which can sometimes be thousands of kilometres long, heading north-east in the northern hemisphere and south-west in the southern hemisphere. Because cyclones systematically follow the same paths, we can identify the areas of the world that are most at risk. The geographical area most affected is the Philippines and the China Sea, where an average of twenty typhoons pass through each year. Next come the Bay of Bengal, in India, with eight cyclones, and the Caribbean and the coasts of western Mexico with six or seven hurricanes, the same amount as those found off Madagascar and near the north-east coast of Australia. In terms of loss of life, the most devastating cyclone in history was Bolha (1970), which killed half a million people in Bangladesh. Katrina (2005) and Harvey (2017), which both hit the US Gulf Coast, caused the most economic damage, estimated at 125 billion dollars.

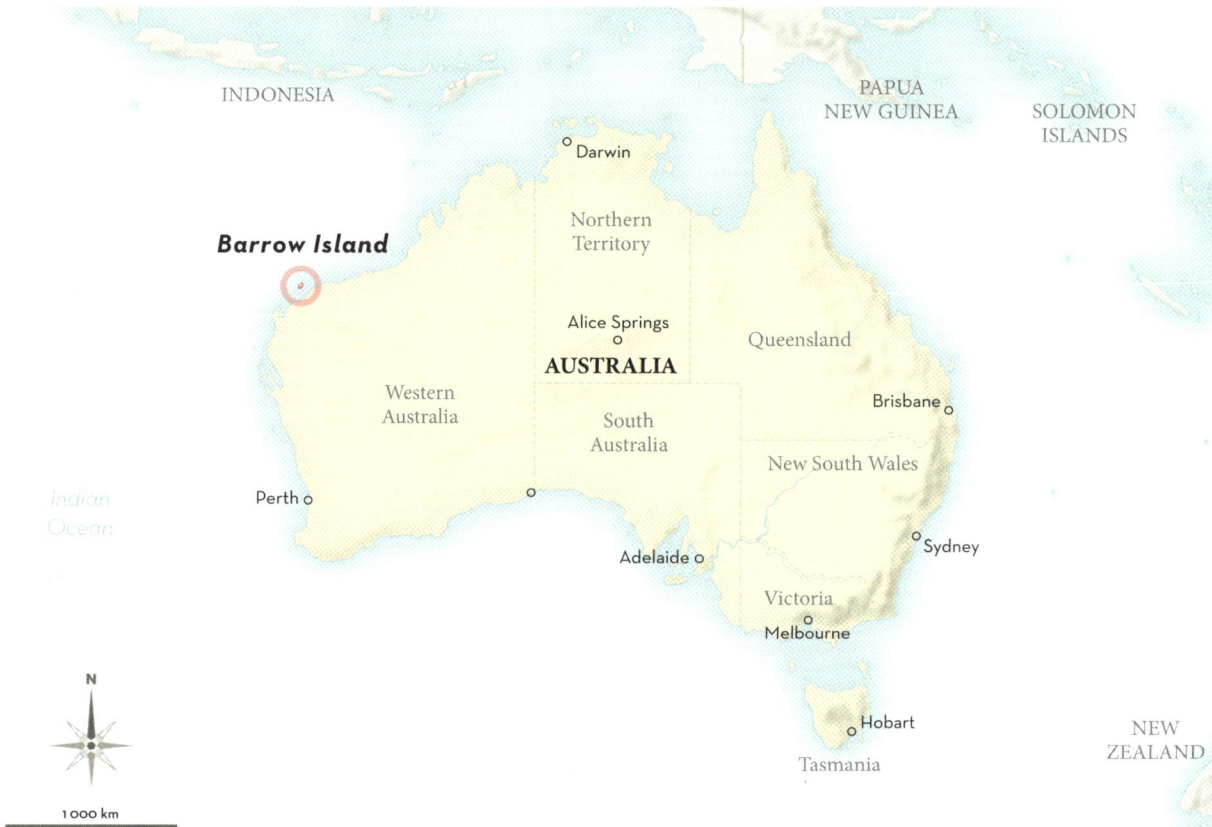

INDONESIA

PAPUA
NEW GUINEA

SOLOMON
ISLANDS

○ Darwin

Northern
Territory

Barrow Island

Alice Springs
○

Queensland

AUSTRALIA

Western
Australia

Brisbane ○

South
Australia

New South Wales

Perth ○

○

Indian
Ocean

Adelaide ○

Sydney ○

Victoria
○
Melbourne

NEW
ZEALAND

N

Hobart ○

Tasmania

1 000 km

Barrow Island – Australia

The highest wind speed ever recorded on Earth

Meteorological history was made on 10 April 1996. The virtually unbreakable record dating back to 1934 of the highest wind speed – 371 km/h on the summit of Mount Washington in New Hampshire, USA – was broken that day.

The 'credit' goes to Olivia, a tropical cyclone that began to form near Indonesia in early April 1996, in the Inter-tropical Convergence Zone between trade winds and monsoon fluxes. Over the next few days, the cyclone moved south-west, growing from category 1 to 4, and deepening off the coast of Pilbara in north-west Australia.

Cyclone Olivia approached Barrow Island with catastrophic power. Its pressure dropped to 925 hPa and wind speeds reached 113 m/s – an impressive 408 km/h.

The World Meteorological Organization only made the record official in 2010 after verifying the functioning of the anemometer. The damage caused by the cyclone was enormous. Oil infrastructures and electricity lines on the island were badly damaged, but no casualties were reported.

There are very few inhabitants on Barrow Island, and it is not open to tourism. The unique history behind the isolation that characterises the island was fundamental in saving it from the devastation cyclone Olivia could have caused.

In fact, Barrow Island is a nature reserve rich in biodiversity, but it also welcomes Chevron Oil's industrial plants linked to the exploitation of an oil field. The combination might seem paradoxical, but it was Chevron that implemented a prudent environmental policy in the 1960s to preserve the numerous animal species on the island. The island's 200 square kilometres is home to some 400 plant species, 13 native mammal species, 110 bird species and more than 44 reptile species, making it one of Oceania's most valuable nature reserves.

© NOAA

ABOUT JONGLEZ PUBLISHING

It was September 1995 and Thomas Jonglez was in Peshawar, the northern Pakistani city 20 kilometres from the tribal zone he was to visit a few days later. It occurred to him that he should record the hidden aspects of his native city, Paris, which he knew so well. During his seven-month trip back home from Beijing, the countries he crossed took in Tibet (entering clandestinely, hidden under blankets in an overnight bus), Iran and Kurdistan. He never took a plane but travelled by boat, train or bus, hitch-hiking, cycling, on horseback or on foot, reaching Paris just in time to celebrate Christmas with the family.

On his return, he spent two fantastic years wandering the streets of the capital to gather material for his first 'secret guide', written with a friend. For the next seven years he worked in the steel industry until the passion for discovery overtook him. He launched Jonglez Publishing in 2003 and moved to Venice three years later.

In 2013, in search of new adventures, the family left Venice and spent six months travelling to Brazil, via North Korea, Micronesia, the Solomon Islands, Easter Island, Peru and Bolivia. After seven years in Rio de Janeiro, he now lives in Berlin with his wife and three children.

Jonglez Publishing produces a range of titles in nine languages, released in 40 countries.

ABOUT THE AUTHOR

Lorenzo Pini is a geographer and author of travel books. Born and raised in Tuscany, he completed his studies in Portugal. He dedicated the guidebooks *A Lisbona con Antonio Tabucchi* (In Lisbon with Antonio Tabucchi) (Giulio Perrone editore, 2012) and *Lisbon, ritratto di città* (Lisbon, portrait of a city) (Odoya, 2013) to the Portuguese capital. In 2015, after a stay in Cuba, he published *Havana, ritratto di città* (Havana, portrait of a city) (Odoya). He collaborated for several years with the publishing house Touring Club Editore, updating texts and itineraries of the *Green Guides* for Portugal (2017), Southern Spain (2019), Denmark (2020) and Tuscany (2021). Pini, who has always been passionate about meteorology and fascinated by weather and climate, writes about it on his blog meteotrip.it.

FROM THE SAME PUBLISHER

Atlas

Atlas of geographical curiosities
Atlas of unusual wines

Photo Books

Abandoned America
Abandoned Asylums
Abandoned Australia
Abandoned churches – Unclaimed places of worship
Abandoned cinemas of the world
Abandoned France
Abandoned Italy
Abandoned Japan
Abandoned Lebanon
Abandoned Spain
After the Final Curtain – The Fall of the American Movie Theater
After the Final Curtain – America's Abandoned Theaters
Baikonur – Vestiges of the Soviet Space Programme
Chernobyl's Atomic Legacy
Clickbait
Forbidden Places
Forbidden Places – Vol.2
Forbidden Places – Vol.3
Forgotten Heritage
Oblivion
Unusual wines
Venice deserted
Venice from the skies

'Soul of' Guides

Soul of Amsterdam – A guide to the 30 best experiences
Soul of Athens – A guide to 30 exceptional experiences
Soul of Barcelona – A guide to 30 exceptional experiences
Soul of Berlin – A guide to the 30 best experiences
Soul of Kyoto – A guide to 30 exceptional experiences
Soul of Lisbon – A guide to 30 exceptional experiences
Soul of Los Angeles – A guide to 30 exceptional experiences
Soul of Marrakesh – A guide to 30 exceptional experiences
Soul of New York – A guide to 30 exceptional experiencess
Soul of Rome – A guide to 30 exceptional experiencess
Soul of Tokyo – A guide to 30 exceptional experiences
Soul of Venice – A guide to 30 exceptional experiences

'Secret' Guides

Secret Amsterdam
Secret Bali
Secret Bangkok
Secret Barcelona
Secret Belfast
Secret Berlin
Secret Brighton – An unusual guide
Secret Brooklyn
Secret Brussels
Secret Buenos Aires
Secret Campania
Secret Cape Town
Secret Copenhagen
Secret Dublin – An unusual guide
Secret Edinburgh – An unusual guide
Secret Florence
Secret French Riviera
Secret Geneva
Secret Glasgow
Secret Granada
Secret Helsinki
Secret Istanbul
Secret Johannesburg
Secret Lisbon
Secret Liverpool – An unusual guide
Secret London – An unusual guide
Secret London – Unusual bars & restaurants
Secret Los Angeles
Secret Madrid
Secret Mexico City

Secret Milan
Secret Montreal - An unusual guide
Secret Naples
Secret New Orleans
Secret New York – An unusual guide
Secret New York – Curious activities
Secret New York – Hidden bars & restaurants
Secret Paris
Secret Prague
Secret Provence
Secret Rio
Secret Rome
Secret Seville
Secret Singapore
Secret Sussex – An unusual guide
Secret Tokyo
Secret Tuscany
Secret Venice
Secret Vienna
Secret York – An unusual guide

Secret Washington D.C.
Secret York - An unusual guide

Follow us on Facebook, Instagram and Twitter

Cartography: **Cyrille Suss** – Translation: **Olivia Fuller** – Layout: **Emmanuelle Willard Toulemonde** –
Copy-Editing: **Lee Dickinson** – Proofreading: **Kimberly Bess** – Publishing: **Clémence Mathé**

Cover photo: © **User9637786_380 / iStock 1251227757**

© JONGLEZ 2023
Registration of copyright: September 2023 – Edition: 01
ISBN: 978-2-36195-699-8
Printed in Slovakia by Polygraf